To Rev. Huntley & Mrs Huntley Dec. 16, 2014

Enjoy it ;

... With love

from - Moetis

SOUTH AFRICAN TREASURY OF POEMS & PROSE

MOITSADI MOETI Ph.D.

authorHOUSE®

AuthorHouse™
1663 Liberty Drive
Bloomington, IN 47403
www.authorhouse.com
Phone: 1-800-839-8640

© 2012 by MOITSADI MOETI Ph.D. All rights reserved.

No part of this book may be reproduced, stored in a retrieval system, or transmitted by any means without the written permission of the author.

Published by AuthorHouse   03/02/2012

ISBN: 978-1-4685-4903-4 (sc)
ISBN: 978-1-4685-4902-7 (hc)
ISBN: 978-1-4685-4901-0 (e)

Library of Congress Control Number: 2012901850

Any people depicted in stock imagery provided by Thinkstock are models, and such images are being used for illustrative purposes only.
Certain stock imagery © Thinkstock.

This book is printed on acid-free paper.

Because of the dynamic nature of the Internet, any web addresses or links contained in this book may have changed since publication and may no longer be valid. The views expressed in this work are solely those of the author and do not necessarily reflect the views of the publisher, and the publisher hereby disclaims any responsibility for them.

Contents

ACKNOWLEDGEMENTS

The author would like to thank the following for their permission to use copyright material: Wole Soyinka for Ogun Abibiman 1. Induction, After the Deluge, Apologia (Nkomati), and 'No!' He Said; President Mandela's office for Letters written by Mandela during his Incarceration on Robben Island Tim Couzens for Dhlomo The New African: A study of the life and work of H.I.E.

The University of South Africa for Arthur Nortje: Waiting The author has made every effort to trace copyright holders, but in some cases without success. We shall be very glad to hear from anyone who has been inadvertently overlooked or incorrectly cited and make the necessary changes at the first opportunity.

INTRODUCTION

In the presentation of my work I opted to use the term *Bantu* to signify indigenous aborigines of the country of South Africa. That is, Bantu people are those not introduced from other countries but are native to South Africa. The "Wananji" of South Africa's ancestral abode since time immemorial.

This material (Prose and Poems) presented by the author derives from a concern with the paucity of contemporary South African literary works and poems by Bantu scholars. It delves into the narrative experiential history of the region because otherwise it would be impossible to understand how the present came into being and what the trends are for the post-Apartheid South Africa. Thus, the material aims to also present the historical events that shaped South African literary works and poetry written in English. Unlike previous anthologies, my poems do not include translations from other languages, nor does the writing pretend to be comprehensive either in terms of one particular ethnic group within South Africa or of the continent as a whole. To bring back the memory of the indigenous aborigines of South Africa and their lost pride is the task of my poems. I have attempted to do this by including the work of the first major indigenous Bantu poet and playwright, Herbert Dhlomo. As a consequence of my interest in corrective literary works, I focused on presenting my work written in the perspective of South African experiences and unique in style but, there is also an attempt to achieve a trend common to African writers responding to their immediate environment. That is why some historical events, especially written by President Nelson Mandela have been given more space than others, and why entire works north of South Africa have been omitted altogether. President Mandela's work is presented in order to give the reader a sense of understanding the development of his magnificent oratory, and literary talent; more especially of presenting such literature under the most oppressive conditions of the Apartheid regime. Indeed, President Mandela's work and letters are capable of educating and influencing the minds of those familiar and unfamiliar with South African history.

My poems are intended to reveal Apartheid's most notorious strategy of dehumanizing the indigenous Bantu population. Nevertheless, the political presentation, devoted to my poems and collection is a reflection of the excellent hope for political positivism, which was found within a tradition of resistance towards the violent nature and the dehumanization of mainly Bantu by the concurrent events under the Apartheid regime. Even a cursory reading of my poems, reveals that *now* is the most opportune time to respond to the conditions that prevailed in South Africa over several decades.

Implicit in my material is the assumption that the reader will explore the integral of bitter memories depicted by the indigenous Bantu. I do so because I believe that this sets my own exposition and conclusions within their proper perspective. Thus, my poems attempt to break the vicious circle of the lack of knowledge about South Africa and brings forward an attempt to reveal the historical events of the region using the literary language and words.

SPEECH AND HURTFUL WORDS
By Moitsadi

A Speech can articulate hurtful words
Which like daggers, pierce my heart
and sing the melody in my pierced muscle and soul
In unison, speech and hurtful words long to devastate
and make me emit red fluid that my heart circulates

Hurtful sharp words with quick strides pierce like daggers
that aim for my hollow heart, their function to dislodge
Shoots to kill, brandishing daggers that cause extreme pain
Leaving my life to languish under words' debilitating harm

Brandishing daggers and hurtful words make me cower
when I remember that these devastating words can
transform even the most stately human being
into a hanging, beaten, destitute spider-cocoon
Barely clinging to the last shreds of sanity
Of precious sanity, seeking but a simple morpheme
that would temporarily refrain from speech

Words of a speech are deft and dexterous yet can
fall trippingly off the tongue with a combination
of sounds that can symbolize the meaning of pain
A speech with supple words and remarks
sometimes made to ease my hurt bounce against
my aching hollow heart causing more pain

But a speech is never satisfied in precise form
until it runs rampant in screams of silent's demise
After the daggers of a speech reach death's final pain
its words brace my soul's core with sworn intentions:
to find that pinnacle of pain immersed in verbiage

Yet words of a speech are my only weapons
And I could use them to tear my foes apart
'cause it sickens me to remember that for centuries
my oppressors used their speech to dehumanize me
Leave me stricken, terrified, desolate, bewildered, broken

I turned out weaker and emptier than I could ever be
when I realized that the sum total of my stability and
humanity was destroyed by my oppressors' curse-words
This exacerbated the pain in my heart and flesh
Shyly my expectant eyes gaze up to heaven
for the confirmation of my hope that these words
could come to an end or put heaven in their tone

My faith in the heaven's judgment and absolute trust
that this peculiar bond between speech and words
will finally heal my bleeding soul to *rehumanize* me and
shed all evil words to heal the pulse in my heart
Have power to stop the daggers from piercing my heart and soul
For I do need a complete obstruction of the pain in my heart

Born to lead. Mandela addressing the United Nations in 1990.

MANDELA: BORN TO LEAD
By Moitsadi

Four score and a dozen years of life
Seared Bantu blood-stains on your soul's doorsteps
Seared red scarlet pangs of sacrifice; recollections
Waiting, anticipating to be a century old
Oppressors tried to drain you until they capitulated
Even in grief they failed to bow you down
Stubborn, you stood where no soul hoped to live
Because you are the one—born to lead

Bantu children's screams enraptured, you heard
They'll celebrate the adulthood of South Africa's democracy
They'll add ten years to each year you spent on Robben Island
One thousand to each trillion moments you could have had
With Zindzi, Zeni, Zami and Us; families with exacerbated nerves.
Moments you should have had with all peace-lovers
Not casting crimson colors past the shadows of blood—
Bantu children's red blood. Your kith and kin's blood
Watering the trees of freedom from Apartheid's terror
Indeed *with their blood they did water the trees of freedom*
Bantu children screened Apartheid's firing line screaming from
Torture, murder, bestial acts; deeds which shrunk the world
Unarmed school-children their pains lavishly outpoured

Waiting anticipating casting crimson in repetition in 1976
During winters on Robben Island away from peace-lovers
You heard Bantu and their children's shadowy voices
You listened to their overtures. echoed their cries
Echoed their rhythms of pain in the dead of night
From the darker stage of twilight as they cry till dawn

While each foe's beat failed to break you
Peace-lovers were killed, others wracked by repercussions
But Bantu and their children's tears will come in the rain
We will name each tear after you Mandela
Yea, name them for you Mandela and
In prayer their tears in our cupped hands we'll honor

Taught by you, Mandela this *Ubuntu* magic we know
You always play to capture the enemy king and win
You did not surrender it was naught for their pawns
Because you were born with a will to fight and win
For what is right and conformable to justice
Peaceably, in spirit of unity you united all South Africans

Nurtured in bitter remembrances but too stern for tears
that seemed to sear both blood and soul
While the world's unbroken wall of steel stood still
Refusing to be trodden under Apartheid regime's heel
It was neither for Black nor White, but for Mandela's sake
Noble, staunch and true with *no surrender* in their hearts
Let Justice reign—they all sang,—power to the people

The enemies of progress were howling loudly
at the moon, the cold placid moon
cold noncommittal and unconcerned
because your shine is nature's own and changeless
At last the end-game arrived and now where is
the enemy king? After the middle-game

No place for him to hide, the game is over
Check and mate Mandela, you Mandela have won
While you stood head and shoulders above the crowd
Foes with faces impassive as Halloween masks marvel
Each incarnate sin forgiven, but not obliterated,
Some invisible wrath revealed over *Ubuntu magic*
Foes still implacably and monotonously murmuring secretly
"Truth, Peace and Reconciliation" when Bantu-light flickers

On sinful lanes sunken in wet brown clay and buried forever
Foes in wonderment see and understand *Ubuntu* at last
When from fire to ashes fades their sinful deeds
After twilight bleeding on South African clouds
night creeps in to hide the foes' hateful crimes
A broad way is now paved away from the foes' failed
experiments on Bantu subjects—*other* human beings

But now we must expedite Mandela's glorious successes
And sacrifice to the ancestors in propitiation to appease.
For, Mandela was born with an innate quality to lead
He led the list; our ancestors have done extremely well
For Mandela with his patronizing nod shows that
He approves that the ancestors approve of him because
He was born to lead and he led the list successfully

SON OF BROTHER KUSH

By Moitsadi

Above the deep and dreamless sky
My mother's spirit goes by
While my oppressors sleep
My grandfather's spirit
Watches, son of Kush, with love
The Stranger they will not crown above
No not by my Grandfather
Kush's father
Still fighting traumas and life without justice

No, not as a Stranger
I son of Kush
Shall shed light on life oppressors endanger
Till every cloud is aflame
My deeds will leave my oppressors in shame
Removing sufferings of all the years
Working with love for justice

My mother's ancestors from the sky
Came they to seek her
Her oppressors with their own blood they throttled her
Oh, the separation and transporting rapturous scene
That always comes to my sight
Oh! Grandfather
Kush's father
Fill this my ruptured heart with light
Bring to life the dead, born again
Into the community of peace and justice
Below the skies the Africans from age to age
Their killings they endured
Cleanse your progeny, I son of Kush
Till your truth he sees for sure
Tis not the quest and yearn for retaliations
The oppressors knoweth Africans

Tis not for reparation
That their swords
They take in sorrow
Only need they peace and justice

Tis not as a Stranger
Your word to the utmost, I son of Kush, must know
Oh, my ancestors' spirit in the dreamless sky
Hear me grandfather, Kush's father
Would you let your progeny consider armed revolution?
Even the deaf ear hears and feels the chains of exploitation
For 'tis since the days of yore
Africa's progeny did take hopes in evolution

No, not as a Stranger
will I, son of Kush listen or take heed
but tired of never-ending platitudes,
straight answers do I need

PROTEST AGAINST POLL TAX (1906-1907): THE EVIL THAT WAS

By Moitsadi

"bamba Bhambatha" a call to catch and kill Bhambatha.
South Africa's most savage settlers' brutal repression was
Announced:
'Discipline the Bantu and militarily enforce European rule'
Yelled a commanding military officer at his regiments
Yelling to men who hailed from countries far across the sea
Catch Bambhatha, shoot to kill, catch him dead or alive
Catch Bhambhatha the African giant the greatest?—
never: never, never, never retorted Bantu men of *amabuto*

As the protest by Bantu against Poll Tax marched on
Their glistening brown biceps raised with courage
Their spears and shields kissing their ancestral sky
'Your will shall be done! You *nkosi Bambatha'* sang they
War songs; chanting and humming—filled the air with songs
Bantu men fully charged to fight to the last man
They faced the foreigners without fear and won the battle

In the stealth of night the foreigners staged
a swathe of terror among *aBantu;* killing *voor die voet*
while their militia rounded up hundreds upon hundreds of cattle
and other stock as a deterrent to discipline protesting aBantu
Insurgency flared up and aBantu under Bhambatha killed
European men in the subsequent melee; wounding many more
Obviously, aBantu had once more won a battle that shook the world
A battle to enforce Poll Tax acceptance; but failing miserably

This led to a new crisis for the Europeans who subsequently
Prepared themselves for declared war to enforce Poll Tax acceptance
King *Bambatha*, king of the Lions continued to protest against Poll Tax
introduced to Bantu by foreigners, an unknown system
of national destruction was rejected by the Bantu outright

You Bhambatha with a wave of your shield and spear
mobilized *Impi yamakhanda,* war of the heads
refused to accept and steadfastly stood your ground without fear
To protest and revolt against Poll Tax was uppermost in your mind
Poll Tax? What for? Do what? What is Poll Tax? Cattle for Poll Tax?
Bite your elbow first you *Ernst Dunn, uyinyamazana* you're an animal

The stage was set, *Amandla wetu, Izwe letu*
izinkomo zetu—Abalungu the wizards are the greatest devils
No Poll Tax *asiyifuni,* was the war-cry of the Bantu screaming aloud
Grievances long standing between foreigners' cattle stealing and
Bantu military operations in defense of their country and cattle
facilitated an ominous climate of gloom
as king Bhambatha's anger sparked by killings of Bantu, spilled over

Foreigners are killing our nation, our wives and children for Poll Tax
foreigners are not people they are wild animals, Bambatha extolled
Bulalani abalungu bafunani lapa, izwe letu let them to the sea return
buyelani kwenu to countries of your forefathers and their forefathers
to countries without cattle. We the Bantu are rich we have cattle
Bhambhatha declared as he pulled a tree-branch, flung it to the ground

Pounded on the branch angrily with his left foot as a symbol of disgust
His right hand shaking his shield rhythmically.
"Foreigners are cowards, *Bulalani Izinyamazana*
kill all *abalungu* the wild animals. Foreigners in our land"

He gave instructions, how dare these foreigners; these wild bats
introduce Poll Tax, how dare they take thousands and thousands of
    our cattle
the gods of our abode. Killing us for Poll Tax? Stealing our cattle?
Bhambatha asked and gave command: Kill the cattle-thieves
Destroy the bats wherever they tread, *izwe letu* they must go away
They who fly by night and sleep during the day: cowards without cattle
Izwe letu they are forbidden to step on our grass and soil
Leave us alone you foreigners with uncooked pink
skins and features like those of pigs ready to be skinned
and roasted on fires for our ancestors to witness the wizards on fire

Thus, hatred against an unknown hideous poison—Poll Tax
Poll Tax System of destruction—Poll Tax, phrase uttered with disgust
Words without *Bantu* equivalents—words that spell doom like
huge stones lodged down throats of *Bantu* with unimaginable pains
Bhambhata continued, sat on a rock, the crowd shouting and dancing
A war-dance depicting anger, *Bayete nkosi, wena nkosi, Bayete, Bayete!*
Your law shall be fulfilled, no Poll Tax, the foreigners must depart
No foreigners in our midst, your noble and staunch truth shall remain

Gobizembe said with a powerful voice seconded by *Mpanza*
Notwithstanding *abalungu* must leave our country for good
Trace the path you travelled—pack your boots and go back
Follow instinctively the sea-route of the *Goedehoop*
Follow instinctively the sea-route of the *Dromedaris*
Follow instinctively the sea-route of the *Ruiger*
Names Named—their names innumerable these ships
That brought people who hailed from across the sea
With their vast horde and cargo bring they shame

Perhaps the *Bantu World* without foreigners
Without Poll Tax will bring back Africa's glory
Bambatha informed his people.
Throw them into the sea, they are meals for the sharks
Bulala bonke abalungu. Bulalani bulalani inyamazana
Izwe letu, inkomo zetu, Izwe la Bantu. No Poll Tax, no Poll Tax

Take and Keep the Poll Tax in your countries overseas
Makubenjalo!! We do not want you here. We do not want Poll Tax.
Izwe Letu: Sofasonke, Sofasonke! What song shall be worthy to sing
when all the foreigners are no more.
Izwe Letu, no Poll Tax. We *aBantu* the next morning shall sing
Makubenjalo, makubenjalo, kude kube kunaphakade

PEACE IS BUT A PRAYER
MANDELA
By Moitsadi

Mandela always knew that someday
He would once again feel
The grass under his feet
And walk in the sunshine
A free man. He continued
Quote unquote:
"In judging our progress as individuals
We tend to concentrate on external
Factors such as one's
Social position, influence and
Popularity, wealth and standard
Of education . . .
But internal factors may be even
More crucial in assessing one's
Development as a human being:
Honesty, sincerity, simplicity,
Humility, purity, generosity
Absence of vanity, readiness to serve
Your fellow men—qualities within
The reach of every soul
Prisoners cannot enter into contracts.
I cannot and will not give any understanding
At a time when I and you, the people,
Are not free.

We who are confined within the grey
Walls of the Pretoria regime's prisons
Reach out to our people.
With you we count those who have perished
By means of the gun and the hangman's
Rope. We salute all of you—
The living, the injured, and the dead
For you have dared to rise
Up against the tyrant's might . . .

We face the future with confidence.
For the guns that serve Apartheid cannot
Render it unconquerable.
Those who live by the gun
Shall perish by the gun.
Unite mobilize! Fight on!
Between the anvil of united mass action
And the hammer of the armed struggle
We shall crush apartheid and
White minority racist rule.
Amandla Ngawethu! Matla ke a Rona!

As we entered the new decade my hopes
For South Africa rose once again.
Some mornings I walked out
Into the court-yard and every
Living thing there, the seagulls,
The wagtails, the small trees,
And even the stray blades of grass
seemed to smile and shine in the sun.
It was at such times when I perceived
the beauty of even this small, closed-in
corner of the world, that I knew
that some-day my people and I would
be free. Your freedom and mine
Cannot be separated.
I will return.

I am not prepared to sell the birthright of
the people to be free.
I cherish my own freedom dearly,
But I care even more for your freedom.
Too many have died since.
Too many have suffered for the love of freedom.
I owe it to their widows. To their orphans,
To their mothers and to their fathers
Who have grieved and wept for them.
Not only I have suffered during these long,
Lonely, wasted years. I am not less-loving
Than you are. But I cannot sell my birthright,
Nor am I prepared to sell the birthright of
the people to be free. I am in prison as the
Representative of the people and of
your organization, the African National Congress,
Which is banned.

Only free men can negotiate.
Prisoners cannot enter into contracts.
I cannot and will not give any understanding
At a time when I and you, the people,
Are not free. Your freedom and mine cannot
Be separated. I will return".

Above and following page: Mandela on the campaign trail and (right) casting his vote on election day at Ohlange High School near Durban. Mandela chose to vote near the grave of John Dube, one of the founders of the ANC.

Mandela: **Stand up Bantu**, our world shall never pass away.

UTATA MANDELA
By Moitsadi

Mandela's Statement

"When I was a boy brought up
In my village in the Transkei
I listened to the elders of the tribe
Telling stories of the good old days
Before the arrival of the white man
Then our people lived peacefully
Under the democratic rule
Of their kings and their *Amaphakati*
And moved freely and confidently
Up and down the country
Without let or hindrance then
The country was ours
In our own name and right" SAID utata Mandela.

RESPONSE
By Moitsadi

Nonetheless, now for all we have and are
With our heads heavy and hot but not yielding.
For all our children's sake our heads shall forget
their heaviness. Stand up Bantu and remind your foes
Thebe ya sera and Umkhonto we sizwe are at the gate
To defend against the evil that lurks all around our country

Our world shall never pass away, for
They defend against the foe's implacable fury
That might torture our kith and kin.
On our ancestors' heads we swear
We'll never more be strewn in bloody clots
To be carrion of rats and worms. Never more.

NELSON MANDELA, OCTOBER 22,1962

By Moitsadi

"Why is it that in this courtroom I am facing
A white magistrate, confronted by a white prosecutor
Escorted by white orderlies?
Can anybody honestly and seriously suggest
That in this type of atmosphere the scales
Of justice are evenly balanced?

Why is it that no African in the history of this
Country has ever had the honor of being tried
By his own kind by his own flesh and blood
I am a black man in a white man's court
This should not be!" ASKED utata Mandela

RESPONSE
By Moitsadi

Cool upon his brow when for once
The courtroom was quiet, the quiet of the atmosphere
Like the gentle heat that broods on cold waters
Mandela hovered gently and brooded
As he scanned the courtroom
People waited, placid but inwardly on fire
He had never seen so many united startled eyes before
Black eyes, yellow eyes, green eyes, blue eyes, brown eyes
Along nature's continuum. Others in between

Glued all on his cool brow, although, of course
He had known that there were millions upon millions
Of eyes the world over watching, waiting, and watching
He'd never realized that eyes also count for so much.
He had never doubted people's hope. He saw hope scribbled
All over the faces of human beings, beaming in similitude
It was queer, the things eyes and hope taught him

He had wanted to try and count the faces, the eyes, the ears
The eyes shone so bright and clear, the message so clear
All extolling in unison, 'let justice prevail, justice, justice
Justice must prevail'
A simple harmonic motion built into their hearts.

Neither Black nor White. From right to left: Mandela, de Klerk and Buthelezi.

Mandela and Winnie with the Kennedy family in the United States. Around the world.

FROM MOITSADI
To Mandela with love

"NO HE SAID"
Wole Soyinka

Shorn of landmarks, glued to a sere promontory,
The breakers sought to crush his head,
To flush the black will of his race
Back in tidal waves, to flesh-trade centuries,
Bile-slick beyond beachcombing, beyond
Salvage operations but—no, he (Mandela) said.

Sea urchins stung his soul. Albino eels
Searched the cortex of his heart,
His hands thrust high to exorcise
Visions of lost years, slow parade of isolation's
Ghosts. Still they came, seducers of a moment's
Slack in thought, but—no, he (Mandela) said.

And they saw his hands were clenched.
Blood oozed from a thousand pores. A lonely
Fisher tensed against the oilcloth of new dawns,
Hand over hand he hauled. The harvest strained.
Cords turned writhing hawsers in his hands. 'Let go!'
The tempters cried, but—no, he (Mandela) said.

Count the passing ships. Whose argosies
Stretch like golden beads on far horizons? Those are
Their present ease, your vanished years. Castaway,
Minnows roost in the hold of that doomed ship
You launched in the eye of storms. Your mast is seaweed
On which pale plankton feed, but—no, he (Mandela) said.

Are you bigger than Nkomati? Blacker
Than hands that signed away a continent for ease?
Lone matador with broken paddle for a lance,
Are you the Horn? The Cape? Sequinned
Constellation of the Bull for tide-tossed
Castaways on pallid sands? No, he (Mandela) said.

The axis of the world has shifted. Even the polar star
Loses its fixity, nudged by man-made planets.
The universe has shrunk. History reechoes as
We plant new space flags of a master race.
You are the after-burn of our crudest launch.
The stars disown you, but—no, he (Mandela) said.

Your tongue is salt swollen, a mute keel
Upended on the seabed of forgotten time.
The present breeds new tasks, same taskmasters.
On that star planet of our galaxy, code-named Bantustan,
They sieve rare diamonds from moon dust. In choice reserves,
Venerably pastured, you . . . but—no, he (Mandela) said.

That ancient largesse on the mountaintop
Shrinks before our gift's munificence, an offer even
Christ, second-come, could not refuse. Be ebony mascot
On the flagship of our space fleet, still
Through every turbulence, spectator of our Brave New World.
Come, Ancient Mariner, but—no, he (Mandela) said—

No! I (Mandela) am no prisoner of this rock, this island,
No ash spew on Milky Ways to conquests old or new.
I (Mandela) am this rock, this island. I toiled,
Precedent on this soil, as in the great dark whale
Of time, Black Hole of the galaxy. Its maw
Turns steel-wrought epochs plankton—yes—and
Vomits our new worlds.

In and out of time warp, I (Mandela) am that rock
In the black hole of the sky.

THE BEST PART OF THE NATURE OF HUMAN NATURE

By Moitsadi

Mandela's childhood reflections

I

Thinking about you and home does me lots of good
For most of the time such thoughts give me plenty of fun
I am able to recall many amusing incidents of my teenage days
One evening the chief stormed out of his bedroom
Dragging a formidable stick to punish Justice
For having forgotten his portmanteau at Umtata
Cenge, beside whose car we stood jumped to the wheel
And raced away at top speed whilst Justice took to his feet
And vanished into the dark night. I was not involved
So I thought, and remained standing where I was
But as the chief approached, I realized that
I had been left to handle the baby "I am not Justice"
I loudly protested, came back the terrifying retort
"You are!" You know the rest of the story

Then there was the unforgettable occasion when you scolded me
for stealing green *mealies (corn)*from Rev. Majola's garden
that evening the chief was indisposed and you conducted
the family prayer. We had hardly said "*Amen*"
when you turned to me and boomed: "Why do you
disgrace us by stealing from a priest?"
I had a perfectly straight forward answer namely
That stolen food was to me far more sweeter
Than all the lovely dishes I got effortlessly from you
But the way you timed your unexpected rebuke
Made me speechless, I felt that all the angels
Of heaven were listening, horrified by my infernal

Crime never again will I temper with the property
Of clergymen, but *mealies* from the garden
Still continued to tempt me. There are dozens of such incidents
which I like to recall in the solitude of my cell

But why should I yearn so much for you? There are times when
my heart almost stops beating, slowed down by heavy loads
of longing, I miss you, *umqekezo* and its people.
I miss *Mvezo* where I was born and *Qunu* where I spent
The first ten years of my childhood. I long to see Iyalara
Where Justice, Mantusi, Kaizer and I underwent
The traditional rite of manhood. I would love to bathe
Once more in the waters of *Umbashe,* as I did at the beginning
Of 1935 when we washed off *ingceke.* When will I again
See *Qokolweni,* and Clarkebury, the school and institution
Which enabled me to see the distant and dim outlines
of the world in which we live . . . . Above all I miss *Ma*
with her kindness and modesty. I thought I loved her
when she lived
But it is now that she is gone that I think I could have
Spent more time to make her comfortable and happy
You know what I owe to her and the chief. But how and with
What could a prisoner pay a debt owed to the deceased?

FRIENDS IN NEED, FRIENDS INDEED

By Moitsadi

Extract from a letter written by Mandela to Amina
Cachalia from his cell in Robben Island dated 1969

II

Exactly where do I start in writing to you Behn
Aug '52 in Aggie's flat where you cooked pigeons
For Yusuf and me the night before we appeared in court
With Flag and others and when I discovered for the first
Time that you and Yusuf were united by firmer and more
Intimate ties than politics offer? Nei, that would take us back
into history. The night in the late fifties when we saw
"The 10 Commandments"? Perhaps it may be better
To remind you of the tasty curry dishes you
Brought to Chancellor House when I worked there under
Police escort during the 1960 state of emergency.
I well remember how one evening you came with refreshments
to the Square which in turn a cop carried to my cell
"Your wife?" he asked almost in a whisper. "No my sister"
I replied. Come March '61 the day the Treason Trial ended
You were amongst those who travelled all the way to Pretoria
Who warmly congratulated and cheered us on our discharge
Glad to share the victory with those with whom you had
Fought so hard and long for a new order and a new world.
Zami and I met you at a party the same night but you were
Soon gone. A few days thereafter I bade farewell to Zami
And kids and now I'm a citizen across waves. It was
not an easy decision to make. I knew the hardship, misery,
humiliation to which my absences would expose them
I have spent anxious moments thinking of them and have
Never once doubted Zami's courage and determination
But there are times when I even fear receiving letters from her,
Because on every occasion she comes down, I see with

My own eyes the heavy toll on her health caused by the
Turbulent events of the last eight years.
Moments in my life are occupied by tormenting thoughts of
This kind. But most of the time I live in hope and high spirits
As I think of the progress we are making in the sphere of ideas
And in important other directions and the golden friends
Whose sacrifice at one time or other make these advances possible
They give us the strength and courage to continue
Striving for what is permanent in the values for which mankind
Has fought right down the centuries. It is against this
background that we think of you Amina. Few of us are
likely to forget the forties and the fifties when you were
right in the forefront of the youth and women's movements
Indifferent health slowed down your tempo and took away
some of the fire that was once in you. But yours is a past you
cannot shake away, from your life, it is part and parcel
of our history. I think of you with pride and fond memories

III

I write to give you, Kgatho and Maki my deepest sympathy.
I know more than anybody else living today just how devastating
This cruel blow must have been for Thembi was your first born
And second child that you have lost. I am also fully conscious of the
Passionate love that you had for him and the efforts you made
To train and prepare him to play his part in a complex modern
industrial society. I am also aware of how Kgatho and Maki
adored and respected him, the holidays and good time
they spent with him in Cape Town . . . . throughout the last
five years up to March this year. Nobandla gave me interesting
accounts of his attachment and devotion to the family and the personal
interest he took in all his relatives. I last saw him five years ago
during the Rivonia Trial and I always looked forward to these
accounts for they were the main channel through which I was
able to hear something of him.
The blow has been equally grievous to me. In addition to the fact
That I had not seen him for at least sixty months. I was neither
Privileged to give him a wedding ceremony nor lay him
to rest when the fatal hour had struck

The Commanding Officer
Robben Island

Letter from Mandela to the commanding officer
of Robben Island requesting permission to attend Thembi's
Funeral, dated July 22, 1969. The request was subsequently denied.

IV

My eldest son, Madiba Thembekile, aged twenty four
Passed away in Cape Town on June 13, 1969,
As a result of injuries he sustained in a motor-car accident

I wish to attend, at my own cost, the funeral proceedings
And to pay my last respect to his memory. I have
no information as to where he will be buried,
but I assume that this will take place either in Cape Town,
Johannesburg or Umtata. In this connection I should be pleased
If you would give me permission to proceed with or without
Escort, to a place where he will be laid to rest.
If he will already have been buried by the time you receive
This application then I would ask that I be allowed to visit
His grave for the purpose of "laying the stone" the traditional
Ceremony reserved for those persons who miss
The actual burial.

It is my earnest hope that you will on this occasion find it
Possible to approach this request more humanely than
You treated a similar application I made barely ten months ago
In September 1968, for leave to attend my mother's funeral.
Approval of the application would have been a generous
act on your part, and one which would have made
a deep impression on me. Such a humanitarian gesture
would have gone a long way in softening the hard blow
and painful misfortune of an imprisoned man losing a mother
and would have afforded me the opportunity to be present
at the graveside. I might add that I last saw my late son
a little more than five years ago and you will readily
appreciate just how anxious I am to attend the funeral.

Finally I would like to point out that precedents exist
when governments have favorably considered
applications of this nature.

<h1 style="text-align:center">V</h1>

I write on behalf of Mummy and myself to
Give you deepest sympathy. All of us were very
Fond and proud of Thembi and he, in turn was devoted
To us, and it is indeed very sad to think that we will never
See him again. I know just how he loved you. Mummy wrote
To me on March 1 and advised me that he spent his
Holidays with his family in Johannesburg, and that during
that period he took you out several times and gave you much
pleasure and joy. Mummy has also informed me that he had
invited you to spend the forthcoming December holidays
with him in Cape town and that you were looking forward
to a lot of fun. There you would have seen the sea . . . from
the top of the mountain you would see Robben Island across
the waves.
It was not possible for Mummy and myself to attend his funeral.
Both of us are in jail and our request for permission to go to
The funeral was not granted. You also did not attend, but
When you return from school Kgatho will arrange for you to see
The grave and bid your departed brother farewell.
Perhaps one day Mummy and I will be able also to
Visit the grave. But now that he is gone, we must forget about the
Painful fact of his death. Now he sleeps in peace, my darlings,
Free from troubles, worries, sickness, or need; he can feel
Neither pain nor hunger. You must continue with your
Schoolwork, play games and sing songs.

This time I have written you a sad letter. On June 23 I had written
you another letter which was just as sad, because it deals with the arrest
of Mummy. This year has been a bad one indeed for us but happy
days will come when we will be full of joy and laughter. What is even
more important is that one day Mummy and I will come back and
live happily together with you in one house, sit at table together,
help you with the many problems you will experience as you grow.
But until then Mummy and I will write to you regularly. Tons and tons
Of love my darlings.

Affectionately
Tata

VI

I believe that on December 1 you and 21 others
Will appear before the Pretoria Supreme court
On a charge of the Sabotage Act, alternatively
For contravening the provisions of the suppression
Of Communism Act. I am informed that you have
all instructed Mr. Joel Carson to act in the matter . . .

Since our wedding day in June 1958 you have, under
some pretext or other, ben dragged three times before
the Criminal Court and once before a Civil one.
The issues involved, at least, in part of this litigation
Are better forgotten than recalled. They caused us
Much grief and concern. This will be the 5th occasion,
And I suspect that here there is much that lies beneath
The surface, and the proceeding are likely to be the
Bitterest experience of your entire life to date.
There will be those whose chief interest will be
To seek to destroy the image we have built over
the last decade. Attempts may be made to do now
what they have repeatedly failed to achieve
in former cases.
I write to warn you in time of what lies ahead to enable
You to prepare yourself both physically and spiritually
To take the full force of the merciless blows that I

feel certain will be directed systematically at you
from the beginning to the end of the trial, in fact
the trial, and the facts and the circumstances surrounding
it, may so far influence your thoughts and actions
that it might well constitute a landmark in your
entire career, compelling you to re-examine very carefully
values you once fondly cherished and to give up pleasures
that once delighted your heart, ...

. . . I do wish you to know that you are the pride of my heart
And with you on my side, I always feel I am part of an
Invisible force that is ready to win new worlds. I am confident
That, however dark and difficult times might seem now
One day you will be free and be able to see the beautiful
Birds and lovely fields of our country, bathe in its marvelous
Sunshine and breathe its sweet air. You will again see
The picturesque scenery of the land of Faku, where your
childhood was spent and the Kingdom of *Ngubenqcuku*
where the ruins of your own kraal are to be found.

I miss you badly! Tons and tons of love
and a million kisses.
I think of your mother who must have been
severely shocked to lose a son so early in his life
and who had already begun to take over some of
the heavy duties of a parent that will now press
on her from all sides. I think more particularly
of you and Maki because I realize fully how
hard a blow Thembi's death must have been to
both of you. He sincerely loved you, and you, in
turn, were very fond of him. He was not just a
brother, but a person to whom you naturally
turned for advice and assistance. He was the
shield that protected you, against danger, and
that helped you to build the self-confidence
and courage you need to deal with the numerous
problems that you meet as you grow . . . .

I think it proper to highlight but one
Striking virtue of his which created a deep
Impression on me. His love and devotion to you,
Maki, Zeni, and Zindzi and to relatives
Generally created the image of a man who
Respected family ties and who was destined to
Play an important role in the upbringing,
Education and development of the children. He
Had already developed himself to a position
Where he had become the object of his sisters'
Love, admiration, and respect and a source of
Pride to the family. From 8115 I was kept
Constantly informed of his un-flagging interest
In all of us and details of his hospitality during
His recent visit with his family to Johannesburg
Were outlined. The late Fanny never missed the
Chance of saying something complimentary
About him whenever she visited me here, and I
Sincerely regret that death has denied him the
Opportunity to bring this magnificent gift of his
In full play in the service of the family.

VII

I hope you received the Xmas card I sent you
And Kgatho and that you enjoyed your Xmas
And new year. It was a real pleasure for me to
Get your undated letter in November 1967.
The language and style were good and the writing
Clear. It pleased me very much to hear that you
were enjoying yourself in school and that you
Liked English the best. I was also happy to know
that your ambition is to become a doctor
or scientist. Both are strenuous professions and you
must work hard and steadily during school
terms and have a good rest during school holidays.
I see that you are afraid of being kidnapped
One day when you have discovered a dangerous drug
Do not worry much, about kidnappers.

Their world is getting smaller and smaller
And their friends fewer.
One day there will be a new world when all of us
Will live in happiness and peace.
That world will be created by you and me
By Kgatho, Zeni, and Zindzi: by our friends
And countrymen.
When you become a Doctor or scientist
And you use your knowledge, training and skill
To help your people who are poor and miserable
And who have no opportunity to develop,
You will be fighting for that new world.

Extract from a letter written by Mandela to his
Daughter Makaziwe, dated February 16, 1969
But not send until after Thembi's death.
When it was updated on July 29, 1969.

It is more than eight years since I last saw you
And just over 12 months since Mummy was
Suddenly take away from you.

Last year I wrote you 2 letters—one on the 23rd June
And the other on the 3rd August. I now know that you never
Received them. As both of you are still under 18,
And as you are not allowed to visit me until you
Reach that age, writing letters is the only means
I have of keeping in touch with you . . . . The mere fact of writing
Writing down my thoughts and expressing my feelings
Gives me a measure of pleasure and satisfaction . . . .

. . . I last saw our brave and beloved Mummy in December 1968
She was arrested on the 12th May last year about 2 weeks
Before she was due to visit me. Her visit brought me
Joy and inspiration and I always looked forward to them
I must confess that I miss her very badly. I also miss you,
Darlings, and hope that you will be able to write me

Nice and long letters in which you
You tell me everything about yourselves . . .

I have in my cell the lovely photo that you took during
The 1968 Christmas with the Orlando West High School
In the background. I also have a family photo which
Mummy sent in march 1968.
They make it somewhat easy for me to endure the loneliness
Of a prison cell and provide me with something to cheer
And inspire me every day . . . . Perhaps, one day many years
From now, Mummy will return, and maybe and maybe
It will then be possible for her to arrange for me
To have the little things that are precious to my heart . . . .

The dream of every family is to able to live together
Happily in a quiet and peaceful home where parents
Will have the opportunity of bringing up the children
In the best possible way, of guiding and helping them
Choosing carriers and giving them the love and care
Which will develop in them a feeling of security
And self-confidence. Today our family has been scattered;
Mummy and Daddy are in jail and you live like orphans
We should like you to know that these ups and downs
Have deepened our love for you.
We are confident that one day our dreams will come true;
We will be able to live together and enjoy all the sweet
Things that we are missing at present.

VIII

During the lonely years I have spent behind bars
I sometimes wished we were born the same hour,
Grown up together and spent every minute of our
Lives in each other's company I sincerely believe
that had this been the case I would have been
a wise man. Every one of your letters is a precious
possession and often succeeds in arousing

I have never suspected to be concealed in my being.
In your hands the pen is really mightier than a saber.
Words flow out freely and naturally and common
Expressions acquire a meaning that is at once challenging
And stimulating. The first paragraph of your moving
Note, and more especially the opening line
Shook me violently. I literally felt all the millions of
Atoms take make up my body pulling
Forcefully in all directions. The beautiful sentiments

You have repeatedly urged on me since my arrest
And conviction, and particularly during the last
15 months, are clearly the result more of actual
Experience than of scholasticism.
They come from a woman who has not seen her husband
For almost 2 years, who has been excluded from her
Tender children for more than 12 months and who has
Been hard hit by loneliness, an illness under conditions
Least conducive to recovery, and who on top of all that
Must face the most strenuous test of her life.

I understand perfectly well darling, when you say
You miss me and that one of the few blows
You found hard to take was not hearing from me.
The feeling s mutual, but it is clear that you have gone
through a far more ravaging experience than I have ever had . . . .

What a world of difference to your failing health
And to your spirit, darling, to my own anxiety
And the strain that I cannot shake off, if only
We could meet, if only I could be by your side
And squeeze you, or if I could catch a glimpse
Of your outline through the thick wire netting
That would inevitably separate us . . . .

In spite of all that has happened I have throughout
The ebb and flow of the tides of fortune in
The last 15 months, lived in hope and expectation,
Sometimes I even have the belief that this feeling
Is part and parcel of myself. It seems to be woven
Into my very being. I feel my hope pumping steadily
To every part of my body, warming my
blood and pepping my spirits . . . .

By the way the other day I dreamt of you convulsing
Your entire body with a graceful Hawaiian dance
Of B.M.S.C. I stood one sid of hthe famous hall
With arms outstretched ready to embrace you
As you whirled towards me with the enchanting
Smile that I miss so desperately I cannot explain
Why the scene should have been located at the B.M.S.C.

To my recollections we have been there for a dance
only once on the night of Lindi's wedding reception.
The other occasion was the concert we organized in 1957
When I was courting you or you me I am never certain
Whether I am free to remind you that you took the initiative
In this regard. Anyway the dream was for me a glorious moment.
If I must dream in my sleep, please Hawaii for me . . . .

Keep well my darling, do not allow yourself to be run down
By illness or longing for the children. Fight with all your strength.
Tons and tons of love and a million kisses.

Devotedly Dalibunga

IX

You cross-examined me of my health on Dec 12 . . . .
Don't be disturbed, darling, I hope to outlive Methuselah
And be with you long after you have reached the menopause,
When not even Zeni and Zindzi will fuss over you,
When all the gloss you now have will be gone and your
Body, your lovely face included, will be all wrinkles,
Skin as tough as that of a rhinoceros. I shall nurse
And look after you in every way. Now and then we will
Visit the farm, walk around with fingers of my left hand

Dovetailing with those of your right, watching you
Darting off to pluck some beautiful wild flowers, just as
You did on Sunday March 10 for me. You were dazzling
In that black and white spotted nylon dress.
Every day will be March 10 for me. What does age and blood
Pressure mean to us? Nothing! . . . but you are a witch always
Casting spells on your man . . .

X

I must draw you attention to the abuse of authority,
Political persecution and other irregularities that are being
Committed by the Commanding Officer of this prison and
Members of his staff . . . .

During the last 14 years of my incarceration I have tried to
The best of my ability to cooperate with all the officials
From the Commissioner of Prisons to the Section Guard,
As long as that cooperation did not compromise my principles.
I have never regarded any man as my superior, either in my
Life outside or inside prison, and have freely offered this
Cooperation in the belief that to do so would promote

Harmonious relations between prisoners and guards
And contribute to the general welfare of us all. My respect for
Human beings is based, not on the color of a man's skin
Nor authority he may wield, but purely on merit . . . .

Improper interference with social relationships
My youngest daughter Zindzizwa, sent me
Photographs on 3 different occasions one of
Which I actually saw in my file in 1974
When W/O Du Plessis and I were looking for
The copy of a letter I had written to a former
Minister of justice. When I asked for the photo
He told me we should deal with one thing at a time,
And for that day I left the matter there. When
I subsequently asked for it the photo had disappeared . . . .

I must add that I had no trouble with letters from
My daughters until Zindzizwa complained to the
United Nations about the systematic persecution
Of my wife. Of the 6 I got in 1973 only 3 were
Mutilated. Of the 11 that came in 1974, 7 were
heavily censored and in 1975, 6 out of 16. But
The picture of 1976 totally different. Of the 9
I have received since the beginning of the year
Only one reached me unsullied . . . .

It is futile to think that any form of execution
Will ever change our views. Your government
And Department have a notorious reputation for
Their hatred, contempt, and persecution of
Black man, especially the African, a hatred
And contempt that forms the basic principle
Of a multiplicity of the country's statutes
And cases . . . .

XI

Background
Nelson Mandela considers himself as a leader
of the prisoners on Robben Island and to retain
And improve this image amongst his fellow prisoners,
he, from time to time, acts as a mouthpiece of the prisoners,
by raising the so called general complaints directly
to the Commissioners of Prisons or the Honorable Minister—
the highest authority possible.

Official records are kept of the complaints and requests
by prisoners and the way of disposal and I am quite satisfied
that the head of the prison sees them daily and that we
comply with the provisions as laid down in Regulations 103.
They also have the opportunity to raise their complaints with
the inspectorate when such visits take place.

The International Committee of the Red Cross visited
Robben Island recently and they—including Mandella—
had a golden opportunity to lodge their complaints through
an international organization with the commanding officer;
with senior officers representing Headquarters;
with the Commissioner during an interview between
the Commissioner of Prisons and the delegates of the ICRC
and finally with the Honorable Minister , . .

Before I comment on the various issues raised by him,
I must draw your attention to the introduction of his letter
where he systematically and in a psychological manner brought
the reader under the impression of his own importance,
self-esteem and the very high level at which he as a prisoner
communicates and very clearly creates the impression that
the guards, the head of prison and even the Commanding Officer
are of no importance and not capable of solving his problems

XII

I was informed that you cancelled by study privilege permanently
with effect from 1ˢᵗ January 1978, on the allegation that I abused
the said privilege by using study material to write my memoirs.
I must point out that I was appalled to note that in taking such
a drastic decision, you violated the fundamental principles of
natural justice, and you did not even consider it necessary to

inform me beforehand of the case against me . . . .
In this regard I wish to tell you that you did not at all act in good faith.
Not only did you conceal the fact that you were investigating
an allegation against me, but you also denied me the opportunity
of contradicting any relevant facts which I might have considered
prejudicial to my interests.

It is unlikely that I would have contested my handwriting which appeared
in any material in your possession. But there have been occasion in
the past when some of us have been accused of having abused their study
and privilege on the strength of material which was not in their
handwriting and their study were saved simply because they were able
to establish that the accusation was false. To the best of my knowledge
and belief, neither you nor any of your staff are handwriting experts,
and any opinion you may have on the identity of a particular
handwriting would be quite valueless . . . .

For example if you had given me the opportunity to state my case,
before you withdrew my privilege I might have convinced you that
last year I had no permission to study, and, therefore, could not
have abused any study privilege. This is quite apart from the fact that,
in any case, in the enlightened world of the Seventies, I see nothing
wrong whatsoever in incarcerated freedom fighters writing out their
life-stories and reserving them for posterity. Such privileges have
been granted freely by all sorts of regimes since Roman times.

XIII

We strongly protest against the purpose for and manner in which
the visit to this prison of the local and overseas press and television
men on the 26th April was organized and conducted by the
Department of Prisons. We resent the deliberate violation of our right
to privacy by taking our photographs without our permission, and
regard this as concrete evidence of the contempt with which the
Department continues to treat us.

On the 26th April fellow-prisoner Nelson Mandela was
informed by Major Zandberg that the Minister of Prisons had finally
agreed to the repeated requests by the press to visit Robben Island.
We also learned that the minister had authorized the visit provided
that no communication whatsoever would take place between pressmen
and prisoners.

The minister planned the visit in the hope that it would white-wash
the prisons Department; pacify public criticisms of the Department
here and abroad, and counteract any adverse publicity that might arise
in the future. To ensure the success of the plan we were not given prior
notice of the visit. On that particular day the span from our Section
was given special work of "gardening" instead of pulling out bamboo
from the sea as we normally do when we go to work.

Some 30 liters of milk was placed at the entrance to our Section,
quite obviously to give the impression that it was all meant for us,
whereas in truth we receive only 6.5 liters a day.

Most of us know that a section of the press here and abroad is
sympathetic to our cause and that they would have preferred
to handle the operation in a dignified manner. Nevertheless,
the Minister's disregard for our feelings has led to a situation
where total strangers are now in possession of photographs and
films of ourselves. The impropriety of the Minister's action
is sharpened by the Department's refusal to allow us to take
and send photographs to our own families.

We stress the fact that the way the Minister planned this visit in
no way differs from previous ones. In August 1964 reporters
from "The Daily Telegraph" found that those of us who were
here at the time were "mending clothes" instead of our normal work
at the time of knapping stones with 5lb. hammers. As soon as
the reporters left we were ordered to crush stones as usual.

At the end of August 1965 Mrs. Ida Parker from "The Sunday Tribune"
found us wearing raincoats on our way back from the lime quarry—
raincoats which were hurriedly issued to us at work on the very day
of her visit, and which were immediately taken away when she left.
The raincoats were not issued again until a year later . . . .

At all times we are willing to have press and television interviews,
provided that the aim is to present to the public a balanced picture
of our living conditions. This means that we would be allowed
to express our grievances, and demands freely, and to make comments
whether such comments are favorable or otherwise to the Department.

We are fully aware that the Department desires to present/protect (sic)
a favorable image to the world of its policies. We can think of no better
way of doing so than by abolishing all forms of racial discrimination
by keeping abreast of enlightened penal reforms, by granting us
the status of political prisoners, and by introducing a nonracial
administration throughout the country's prisons.
With few or no skeletons to hide the Department will then no longer
stand in any need for resorting to stratagems . . .

We stress that we are not chattels of the Prisons Department. That
we happen to be prisoners in no way detracts from the fact that we
	are, nevertheless,
South African and Namibian citizens entitled to protection
against any abuses by the Department.

Finally, we place on record that we cannot tolerate indefinitely
any treatment we consider degrading and provocative and, should
the minister continue to do so, we reserve to ourselves the right
to take such action as we deem appropriate.

41

In their rage of hate: Bantu children are easy game.
Soweto, South Africa 1976.

Coffins! Coffins! Coffins! Thousands and Thousands of them.
Bantu Children Killed.
Buried in pre-dug graves . . . Soweto.1976.

THEIR MYTH:
AFRICAN DILEMMA

By Moitsadi

Their myths are so very different from ours
Our myths bring the unknown into relation
with the known through our ancestors
—But they in their myths rejoice in the arbitrary
exercise of bombs and bullets strewn over
Bantu children for days and hours on end
Schizoid in their acts they kneel in prayer
And hide the deep and awful blood-stain
From the blood of Bantu children slain

They narrate their sins and guilt without shame
For killing Bantu children as their game
laughing about it as if they'd won a lottery
in their myths they also grabbed for themselves
that which is another's
Land, beasts, flora, fauna and other Homo sapiens too
They use bombs and bullets to kill Bantu children
What a barbarous method of decimation

In their rage of hate children are easy game for the kill
Moments when their sense of shame they did hide
basking in the shade of the old Apart-Hate
Their faces have lost the blushing in the process of Apart-Hide
they have enjoyed the fruits of Apartheid
and vulgar language from lessons their mothers did teach
Going about it as if they meant to educate their own
What a barbarous myth their lips did utter

In their myths and guilt, the fist clenching
And ferocity of their teeth is displayed
chest-thumping in the image of their gorilla cousins
wild like gorillas as they challenge and defy
the defenseless deafening cry of a child's hurt

Tears drown the children's defenseless prayers
Bantu child begging-"baas, baas, baas that hurts why kill me"
three huge men against a quarter man sjamboked him to death
They've trained each other in the use of bombs, bullets, sjamboks-
"Mama, mama, mama"—running away is the only defense
Laughing about it as if they are making jokes
fulfilling their barbarous myth

Kill *voor die voet* was a battle cry declared—
A war against unarmed Bantu children
And kill they did, to honor their pledge
Where are your children baas in this hour of sorrow?
In school they are indoctrinated in the art of hatred
While you must kill Bantu children for the sake of killing—

Baas—by any standard you are out-barbarized
Lack of civility as you kill defenseless ignorant children
Africa's progeny trying to resist; watered the trees of
liberation, watered trees of freedom with their blood
Bantu children's flesh, blood, bones and shadows of blood
extol dead children's sacrifice to fertilize the trees of freedom

To a deity created in the image of their hate and savagery
which drowns the voice of innocent conscience
is mirrored their prejudice and Apart-Hide
but at Vulindaba and Pelindaba they organized on a massive scale
which magnifies enormously their hatred for Bantu

Their private discourse of Apartheid's evil strategy
obscene in its form it became Apart-hide
ghosts of evil they forget it was Apart-Hate
by the solemn oath of our ancestors we hate to be apart
But their myth—Apartheid, what a name—came to pass
learnt in dumb impious surprise God is not one of
their allies his ways are not their ways

Rainbow Nation. One man one vote; at last 1994.

Baas and Missus no more; Myths of a Superior race no more.

A RAINBOW NATION
By Moitsadi

Why did the Caucasians leave their motherland?
Once more we hear whispers, gossips and ask not
Once more their search away from their countries
was for comfort, content, delight and happiness
Away from communities so poor and pitiful overseas

So manifestly incomplete, their lives crushed
Just perchance industrial revolution
Brought more harm than good—crowded in slums
Their world went mad—lead and steel in factories
did their worst, men, women and children working
underground in coal mines' insecure blundering world
men, women and children working in factories and coal mines
for pittance enough pennies to buy half a loaf of bread

All mangled in slums their tender tissues ploughed away
Away by disease and death torn by the blundering
Disgraceful existence—their king and country
Bade them to leave for green pastures of South Africa
Thus they launched new lives—and great visions
Burst upon their poor, their sick, their lame and others

Peace and fresh air came to them at last
A weary road these foreigners have trod to South Africa
To face the naked truth they shriveled from whence they came
Through perils and dismays renewed and re-renewed
Till all the anguish and pain exploded and angers stirred

To South Africa came they bearing strange ghostly banners
Still telling of something greatly lost in the gloomy somewhere
But now the noise of winds and screams of pain in the coal mines
Are left behind, beyond the utmost pain of their mothers' anguish
To face the new splendor with vigor and new clean attire

Myths of Superior Race, myths of White is Right are no more
now join the Rainbow nation waiting to welcome you
No easy hopes lie in opposite colors to mask your origins
Black and White? no other colors have opposites in life
Neither Black nor White suppositions survive

So vehemently, we scarcely see whence they came
The inner eternal truth of their myths
Who one time had no peace or fresh air
Deep in the belly of their coal mines
They obtruded but traced South Africa's tranquil

For the loveliness of South Africa rich in all things
there is but one task for all South Africans now
This Rainbow Nation must mingle and be one
Even though gazing on South Africa's bosom
We did see pain—Caucasians suckled her bosom
Until it bled, how can Caucasians fleece and strike
Hard yet faced with their Ill-bound countries overseas

Caucasians under South African eaves
conferring drowsily in drunken stupor
from milk and whatever they could bilk.
South Africa bled but wants no recompense
since her waiting dreams are satisfied

The door is still ajar in South Africa
For Europeans way yonder north of Africa
To southern stars of splendor in South Africa
Come in, you are welcome to join
The Rainbow Nation neither Black nor White

Return to dust the dried-leafed wreath
For Black and White vanished myth
Your antagonistic human experiments miscarried
There are no opposites in the Rainbow
Wantonness is overthrown and buried

For all the Bantu and Caucasian's fate
Stand up and salute the Rainbow Nation
—Your world overseas has passed away
There is almost nothing left out there today
In courage cross hearts for strength

To belong to a Rainbow Nation is an honor
enjoy the refreshing sacredness of South Africa
where Uheshani the gleaming South African eagle
Stooped happily down to see truth and reconciliation
Made supreme upon the truth of the matter to reconcile

Uheshani thought his days will drift away with
The coming if the Rainbow Nation
But Alas! Sights and sounds and happy dreams
Of her flight in the sky, she learned
Friends with gentleness in hearts are for peace

A peaceful transition from shame to glee emerged
Hail Truth and Reconciliation Committee
A long name TRC to remember sin and chatter
The same as those with a different charter
And with the dreary, doubtful hours

When the burning awaited moment broke
To announce to the world a newer birth
Where color-wars shall be no more only truth
Great peace, great transition, great rest
And real fullness of life has arrived after dearth

All the bright joyous company of the nation
A rainbow nation stood peacefully together
Each one a blessed friend forever till death
-One prayer: *Amandla Awetu*—must not
be forgotten or denied, this expensive purchase
is a strength that shall not cease to exist

I SPEAK OF MAPUNGUBWE
By Moitsadi

South African *Bantu* deeply humbled!
Indigenous to the marrow of all your bones
Izwe Letu, remember aliens came from across the sea
Pawns that played a bloody game.
Of the pawns were the serfs, the laborers,
The sick, the malnourished and the dying
the poor—the multitudes from overseas
and more of them than any other aliens

Borrowed they from the African game of chess
The oldest and greatest African skill game ever invented
Our ancient bonds with chess still live clearing the minds
of all estranging blindness when Mapungubwe's knights
fought on horseback and challenged the aliens to their game
But after searching fury and torment, shock and pain
The Judge of right and wrong fulfilled Mapungubwe's desires
Never again will the aliens evil spirit loom up

Like the bow of steel Mapungubye stood still
For the glory of Bantu queens and kings
Her toughness is never weakened only triumph exist
Because, Mapungubwe pledged to move the knight
For the rights of Bantu and their full years
that brought incredible equality to inherit

remember whose powerful hand broke Mapungubwe
Barriers of thunder and the fury of lightening were there
Yet alien foes of *Bantu* brought perpetual bitterness and pain
But Mapungubwe's pride surged up within herself on the hilltop
That from the lightening sparks may be springing,
Shooting stars of ancestral heavenly powers to protect
So that with Mapungubwe the light be kindled,

Welling from her ancestral womb
Mapungubwe's gold glow of malleable loving-kindness
Gold stored for veins of Bantu offspring unborn—
From South Africa with love and golden splendor
When Mapungubwe's brow the dust is touching
Prostrate before the ancestral Bantu Queen
South Africa with its latest Bantu Ruler,
Must give Mapungubwe alone all glory,

That her name and words be swiftly filled:
Africa! stretch your hands and outspread
To the ancestral graves on Mapungubwe's hill
Descendants of Bantu's golden land
Comes to us the hidden gold
The honored gift from Bantu's ancestral brow
Of rhinocerus their totem beast carved in gold
Helping to rid the world of myths.

An animal of ancestors, an animal for the Bantu race,
Tshukudu, Rhinocerus full of Wisdom, full of grace,
To be seen and not heard your golden physique
dug from Bantu graves still standing for the right,
Playing your part to explode the great myth.
Bayete Tshukudu Bayete Rhinocerus
Bayete Bayete Hail Hail! you are the greatest

Travelling the path Queen of Mapungubwe trod,
Fear not, as any judge would upon the bench
Reveal your songs which are not exactly hymns
Although they do not miss your ancestral musical fire
And do not include your month of birth, 2000 years ago
Mapungubwe's Queen will save you by Her hand

Keep your swing at an easy pace with her
Never flinching a shade for Bantu race
Africa prays for us and for them, friends and foes
They hid the golden Rhinocerus and other precious cargo
But there you are at last *Tshukudu* and your sight is good
to the eyes of the international world and strewn globally

We thought we will manage to bring you and our cargo
Back to your ancestral graves which shall for ever
Be your permanent home till the end of time
This! an offer we will not refuse

TASTE OF SUGAR
By Moitsadi

There are times when my sweet tooth challenges
the taste of sugar, it is catastrophic this sugar
unknown to the Western World's before 19th century
-Like some dead old vultures we never knew
Came they and tasted Africa's own, nature's own
It was harvest time, the wind was fresh
Rich with the smell of sugarcane when they landed

They caught the smell of sugarcane these people
From across the sea—the Western World—
There was the golden African sun when they saw sugarcane
What is sugarcane? they asked, Buffled, Amazed
Confused by this stock-still twelve foot tall grass cane
Unknown to the Western World

But it is of sugar I wish to speak;
To pin down and lay the lessons learnt
I tease the flesh to reach the nerve and expose
Bo-ammaruri—the truth of the matter
It is the general tissue that I dissect
and then, below this, with attentive eye attempt
to see the faint bloodless nerves of non-Africans
people of the Western World

The grim assertion of some sense of worth
in the teeth that crush the sugarcane for sugar
People of the Western World landed on Africa's beaches
and sand where the brute sense of taste of different fruit
fell unceasingly for this unknown sugarcane
and on the mind that will be the contribution
To the Western World, where sugar was unknown

A simple curiosity is all my woe:
When I only speak of others' greed
those congealed in concrete and damned
by some invisible wrath stronger than
incarnate curse of their rusted backwoods ghettos
in the Western World without sucrose, fructose
lactose without the edible products of perennial grass

Their unarticulated sweet teeth laments
the millions upon millions of uses of sugar
But the stillness said to me, reveal once and for all
What the world would have been without
Africa's sugarcane, without Africa's sugar
Whose presence adorn the tables of royalty
And tables of the poorest of the poor humans
Sugar has become the world's dearest friend
The rich man's dearest friend
The poor man's dearest friend
The sweetest and the best

Sugar! Africa's enormous contribution to the World
When consciousness came back they found between
The opposing minds enquiring what each required
Politely talking weather debating the sweetness of sugar
With one eye open to enslave other humans—Africans
As things turned out they took chances and
Took their luck in life from serfs to slaves they created
Married sugar to slaves for their own profit

TOBACCO—KILLED MY SIBLINGS
By Moitsadi

Sometimes a cloud of ideas is clouded by
A cloud of Tobacco and webs my charged mind,
assenting my delighted dancing mental eye ;
and sometimes the thrust and clash
of stink and unpolished word—Tobacco
make the debate and affirm positively

To the music in the pituitary part of my brain;
My deceased sibling to remember
In noisy continuity of *emphysema* caused by tobacco
Hungry for knowledge I bent my head
The smell of Tobacco fanned my face
My deceased sibling did haunt my memory

Dancing with a measured step from shattered
Lungs and tobacco smoke buried in bronchial tubes
And so devilish the smell that I was never content to smoke
Second-hand, I feel the road to hell unroll before me to keep
my senses straightened toward the goal of destroying tobacco for life

Sometimes a bright and simple statement
stands out unadorned in a haze of good ideas
pleading mutely to be recognized for
an enlightened sympathetic state of bare facts
declaring the evil that tobacco does to mankind

Dark, Dark cigars 4 inches long held between the teeth
As they inhale the rolled product of dangerous value
Dark brown made of chopped broken crushed leaves
that shaded earthworms and snails in fields and yards
Green leaves the color of life below the cuticle
Fresh, hidden to be dried whole for the rich and the poor

The cloudy smoke and the secret never confessed
Cigarettes, snuff to a television that whispered "Danger"
polluting the bright airy untarnished surroundings
with the smoke-woven, cloud-woven, evil-woven air
of pollutants under the ozone layer where we work and live

The blade-edges of the leaves pierce through and through
The cry of the broad edges of rolled dried leaves
from the dark brown masses of the sunlit hedges,
washed by rain water so colorless, and so transparent
as though to remove the blasted stink of tobacco

The menace from the cloud of tobacco smoke
Sharp and clear as the blade of a knife;
and the blade edges of the hedges and shrubs,
gives a piercing pain in the human's wind-pipes
The incisive thrust of polluted air into the lungs
the stinging smoke in the sky and the blinding of the eyes:

From the clear image of the bronchial tubes of the lungs
and air-bubbles gurgling for freedom from lethal
environ glinted with the threat of death.
Caused by the smoke of pleasure and dead ash
Man made and born of Tobacco, death looming ahead
That's the devilish side of Tobacco fascination.
It made my sibling will his own destruction.

Mandela and comrades squatting, crushing stones on Robben Islands.

TO ALL THE COMRADES
By Moitsadi

I remember, I remember, I remember
The vision of Mandela and the comrades
Squatting on the damp sand of Robben Island
Where damp-dust had formed globs on the eaves
There in the dust—smudged in silent fortitude
They hammered and chiseled, hammered and chiseled

There can be little doubt that these several
Minds and spirits stirred by freedom's passion
And energy to fight for liberation—our comrades
Were reacting sensitively both to Apartheid's
Cruelties and to its dehumanizing tactics

These several minds have experienced and displayed
Unselfishness in the face of raging threats
They have silently compared peace conventions
With those undergoing gross exploitation in the world
Though the Apartheid regime did not dare to learn that

Inflexibility of conduct that deadens the spirit
Into a tame submission which cramps
and constrains human beings can never succeed
only the relative spiritual freedom engendered by
re-humanizing fellowmen will heal successfully

Day after day the early morning air and dew
Cling to the hidden window-panes waiting anxiously
For comrades to wake up and begin another day
that usher in the mind-controlling strategies
to shape the minds, to shape the thought processes,
and shape the souls to their extremities of despair:

Prisoners not of war, political prisoners victims
of political strife serving sentences for being human
Not prisoners of war who surrendered to enemy forces
Prisoners taken not during wartime, no declared war but
only demanding liberation—to take back that which is theirs

They endure—while the morning air and wind ripples
Form waves and tides on the surrounding sea-shore
When moist air sprayed and dropped by wind-gusts:
announces the beginning of a different day, another day
Spirits and souls longing to be whole persons to take
and hold and shape forever their countries' destiny . . .

Wounded but not broken in spirit, comrades were still
Sticking it, holding on to sanity lines of bravery
Never a loss of hope, only wounded heads; smashed bones,
Cuts on arms; cuts on feet, sprained ankles, scrapped elbows
fingers in band aids, torn ligaments, bloodied knees:
comrades in bandages wearing a multiplicity of bruises,
but hope not crushed only our wounds they bear for us

On the chopped broken stones all day long they squat
smashing stones into gravel to pave Robben Island's paths
splitting stones with bleeding aching hands missing here and there
another wound splashed open, *"dit is mis, jou gat"*, said the guard
crimson-red was the red blood freshly spilt, (vulgar words ignored)
just shaking the hand to exorcise a spell comrade tried

When the prisoners squatting nearby see the blood
on the gravel they give consolation and say "sorry man
you'll be alright be careful tomorrow is yet another day"
the fresh blood on the fresh grey gravel of Robben Island
sunlit and blown by the airy fresh air from the ocean
and dried by the heat of the sun they still chiseled stones

With bloody hands to form golf ball-sized little stones
the era of the stone-age introduced and reintroduced
not in archaeology class but in practice making stone tools
reinventing the earliest period of human culture in modern times
how vulgar—trying to destroy comrades' minds in the process
yet failing miserably

Rumps scrapped-rough like chisels by sitting on the rocks
The broad edges of a rock in a bloodied hand
shaped to a size ready to be washed around by
swirls of rushing rain-water during stormy weather by
colorless water, transparent and cool with a touch of light:
blood looking crimson-red to light-pink, from gashed wounds

From lacerated wounds still bleeding, the bloody flow
as comrades hobbled through the wet chiseled rocks
avoiding stagnant pools of rain water with feet astride
the thick flow of blood dripping—rain water uncoiling
the skeins of thick dark red mass of blood-clots
to crimson-red a color of table-wine to quench aching souls

The menace of that rainy day whetted their resolute
As they trod from the sharp edges of the rocks,
from the blinding and piercing brilliance of the sun,
to the penetrating thrust of the fresh air into the lungs
from the brightness of glary-sky and eye-blinding light:
To the clear image, of the liberator-Mandela enquiring

Uniformed, in prison garb with his eyes on the next move
on the chess board of politics for he surely was winning
holding his head high and shoulders above all peoples
He bows his head to bless South Africa as dreams come true
And free birds sweep across the heavens and the empty sky
To the ancestral abode murmuring "Freedom! it is done! it is done!"

He raises his head-wide eyed, thanks the ancestral spirit
Nangomso, ke pheto, magubenjalo. Free at last. Oh! Freedom.
Comrades yelled in jubilation. Bantu pulse rates shot up
In disbelieve. Tears of joy rolling down hot cheeks
Ancestors blowing cool air to dry the tears. Wasted moments
Laboring, fighting to be rehumanized. Catching the objectives
and subjective aspects of human nature making history, each
re-echoing Mandela: *it is an ideal for which I have lived.*
It is an ideal for which I still hope to live and see realized,
but if needs be it is an ideal for which I am prepared to die.

Ideal realized! Amandla! Amandla! resounding along the dirt roads
Unpaved roads, paved roads, all roads, dusty pathways and passages
In cities great and small multitudes of people cheering and applauding
All the ancestral graves burst; joyously stood agape as their spirit rose
Unperturbed, undisturbed, unwavering, not agitated but understanding.

A smiling sun gives respect as the ancestral wombs of life conceive
For the Bantu it is an unending Bantu World born to receive
An ideal unbroken for the global world's exercise to perceive
As the ideal began with a peaceful transition never deceived
Each comrade looking up to heaven for the confirmation of their reward
An ideal for which I have lived and realized. They echoed in unison

IZWE LETHU
From Herbert Dhlomo

The glory of our land—deep vales and mountains
The pageantry of flocks gathered near fountains
Of fragrant flowers and herbs, of worms that glow
At night while angels bring us sweet repose
From strife; amorous birds that build their nests
'Mid strains of music, the ancestral guests,
Pie snakes, that speak of our reincarnation
And urge us on to fight for liberation;
Deft scenes of beauty where the weeping willows
Bring rain; where the phantasy of mingled splendor
Of starry nights, sweet sounds, perfume and colour,
Of lizards, bees, blue saes, and winds all sobbing,
And waterfalls, green fields, and birds all soaring,
Combine to make this clime a paradise,
Ah me! Alas! Polluted by the guise
Of those who as they mouth of liberty
And Christian law, shape laws of slavery!

Great Guardian of our shattered Eden fair!
The snake of wrong you challenged without care
Like lovers' kisses so upon our lips
Thy name—which e'en death cannot eclipse

To learn of thee
I rise and flee
My spirit bruised and stiffer,
Would break of treatment rougher.
Divinity come to thee;
O speak and make me free
Accept my shattered offer!

. . . . Time and change are respecters of no person,
Some farmers had bonded their land to money-lenders,
Many of whom were Jews. Others owed large sums to
The benevolent, paternal Government Farmers' bank.
In many farms there were signs of dislocation and poverty.
The farmers were up against the persistent competition
And demands of industry, commerce and the cities.
The gold and coal mines and secondary industries were
Absorbing labour that farmers thought should go to them.
Some of the younger and more ambitious and adventurous
Men and women in the platteland were drifting into the cities.

To protect their interests the farmers had combined into
Agricultural union affiliated to the bigger federal body.
They had also established a recruiting agency.
Farmers with strong individualistic tendencies and those
Who disliked change did not like this. They wanted to be
Left alone as independent masters of their farms and affairs.
They all blamed the various governments of the country
For this state of affairs, and in deference to them
(that is to win their votes) Every government coddled
And pampered them. But they were at a loss whom to blame
For one of their chief sources of trouble—the drought.
In spite of this many farmers made huge profits.
Some of them were influential members of Parliament
And of the provincial Councils. They had cheap labour to
Depend on. These were the vagaries and conflicting trends of farm life.

The frustrated, unrewarded and unrecognized talent and ability
Is one of the most tragic and dangerous things in African life today . . .
Not infrequently, the officials lay this game off against the more
Conservative tribal elements and the Chiefs . . . .
The group certainly is amorphous and divergent in thought
(which is healthy). But it is rooted in and well-versed about
Its tribal and traditional past so that it is not only able to carry
With it the weight of most tribesmen, but to reinterpret
And recreate African culture, and make new forms from it
And graft into the new Culture.

Let me plead with you, lovers of my Africa, to carry with you
Into the world the vision of a new Africa, an Africa reborn,
An Africa rejuvenated, an Africa recreated, young Africa.
We are the light that glimmers of a new dawn.

The African journalist in most cases is underpaid,
Over-worked, is hampered with irritating restrictions
And is not free to speak out loud and bold. Our
Journalists must be and are bilingual—they must
Write in English and Vernacular every week.
They are reporters, sub-editors, editors, proof-readers,
all in one. They are expected to write on every
topical subject under the sun for there is no division of work.

IZINKOMO ZETHU

The inkomo was a link between the world
Of the spirits and of the living, between the past
And the present, the present and the future
Between the known and the unknown, the abstract
And the concrete. The *inkomo* was the means
of offering sacrifice and prayer, a symbol
of appeasement supplication, of reformation
and dedication, purification and atonement.

Now surely must the . . . . *inkomo* lament
For the might and splendor that were
. . . . land lie in ruins, and the power, solidarity
And spelt the . . . . name have deteriorated into
Poverty and vagrancy, and the *inkomo* must,
Like the poetic praises of which the tribal bard
So prophetically spoke, weep among the ruins
Of the dead past, a past that can rise no more,
Rise no more?

Is the past a dead seed that must be trampled under,
Rot and never again live, but forever remain dust;
Or is it alive, ready to germinate and flower forth
Into a radiant and glorious future? Is the . . . . soul dead
And . . . . power forever gone? Or do they lie dazed
In the present winter of national hibernation,
Awaiting the summer smiles and showers of
Self-expressions to bloom forth again in all their
Glory, strength and beauty? Who knows?

The sands of time run outward fast . . .
Out of this flaming past where Shaka's soul abides,
And secret deep confides, to us today, may spring
Again a Force to bring us Name and pride and power
In this afflicted hour

Now from time immemorial
Africa had developed her own peculiar
Plants, animals and men
The African Native or Aborigine
The African Natives then live and move and
Have their being in the spirit of Africa
They are one with Africa
It is then this spirit of Africa which is the common
Factor of co-operation and the basis of unity among
African tribes. It is African Nationalism or Africanism
So that all Africans must be converted
From tribalism to African Nationalism which is a higher
Step or degree of self-expression and self-realization
Of the African spirit. Africa through her spirit
Is using us to develop that higher quality of Africanism . . . .
This African spirit can realize itself through, and be
Interpreted by Africans only

Christmas! How the word and season thrilled us when
We were young. Detribalized, urbanized, Christianized,
We lived and thought as Westerners, and Christmas had
Come to mean to us what it meant to other children
Of European culture. Even the system of education we
Received those days modeled us on similar lines
But most important of all, the English literature we
Read mad us think of Xmas, as of other things
In terms of the British mind and see it through spectacles
Of White authors, British climate, and continental usage.

How we have changed! How we hate ourselves
For having been mere parrots—for having been such plastic clay!
And yet, I fear this same system of training and educating
Our youth (if not a worse) is still going on

We cry, O mystic life or Death of Fate
O what art thou who cannot satiate
Neither our own nor yet thy killing thirst?
In vain we grope last things to know and first
To fathom whence we come and where we go
Knowledge is ours! . . . yet know not what we know!
Where has he gone? We ask in vain—in tears
Today a life he lives transcending years
He's one with things-as-in-themselves=are. We
Behold the shadows, he the Reality;
Ephemeral the thing we shape and see
He is enfolded in Eternity.

The beauty that he loved and sang is one
With him. He is beyond the stars and sun
Mamina, his imagined lve, doth kiss
Him with immortal kisses, not of bliss!
Like Beatrice guide she stands to him who made
Love hermit pure while others love degrade;
Goddess of love, Nomkhubulwana, shakes
His hand, while heaven with music wondrous quakes!
Black bards and heroes greet their friend and peer;
Great shaka, Magolwane there appear,
Mbuyazi, Aggrey, Dube, Mqhayi, ache
To meet him—so Bambatha, his namesake;
Not these alone, for here below he loved
And spoke with long haired bards, among them moved;
Now Keats, his idol, whom he prayed to meet
Chaste Shelley, too, come forth our Bard to greet
And Catholic great Dante, Comedy
Divine enjoying, smiles to meet and see
A Catholic bard mate

Yet seek him there,
You seek in vain. Not vain to seek him here.
For here he lives in mountains and the sea
In birds and falls he sang so beauteously;
Season will come and go, but not your soul
Which caught this panorama inits whole
'the glory is departed!' yet the glory
Still remains in thy victorious crown and story

Then felt we like a barren sour old man
To whom in his despair is given a son
Entranced, we boasted, 'Look! At last, the Sun!'
According to (sic. African) traditional beliefs
The dead return to life in the form of snakes of
Different kinds, the tribal mind was wise enough to
Distinguish between the ordinary snake which is an
Animal and a snake which was a transformed body
Of a dead but living soul. The souls of the dead
Did not enter the ordinary reptiles, but transformed
Themselves into special snakes.

The tribal man believed in the immortality of the
Individual soul. He believed that the living and

The dead had vital connections and interest,
And could communicate with one another
A thing that we have observed, that Psychic research
Is trying to teach and prove today . . . . traditional belief
Taught that the living depended on the dead for many
of their good and ill fortunes. But it went further and
said the dead i.e the Highest and the Holiest
depended on the living for their meaning, position,
and existence. The world of the spirit was only possible
because of the world of the flesh.
One lived and had its being in the other.

O BLOEMFONTEIN,

Fount of flowers;
Bloemfontein,
Fort of ours
What Bantu struggles have your eyes not seen!
For years here hosts of people gathered for
The purpose, keys to find to open the door
To Justice, right, fair law and liberty;
From bondage and from shame to be set free.
First city of the Free State, fount of Flowers,
Not flowers but crowns of thorns are in thy bowers,
For midst thy bounds, the Race has prayed and bled'
And fought to gain the Vision that is fled.
The garden of *Gethsemane* thy name
Will be in the History of the Race. Thy fame
Will be like U'ndi heights or Flanders field
Where heroes, wounded, stood and would not yield,
What fights have not been fought and lost in thee,
O Bloemfontein—grim wars of liberty
Thou art the heart, the centre, the Capital
Of Bantu hopes, fears, throes and strife. Here all
Our giants past and present stood and fought,
And many great campaigns here planned and wrought.
Rejected as the Capital by the whites,
Thou art the Capital of freedoms fights.
Then speak O Bloemfontein and tell the world
Of the tragedy your eyes have seen unfurled;
The tragedy of men against great odds,
Still fighting for *their* children and their gods;
The tragedy of fear, race pride and hate,
That makes a mockery of thy name—Free State.
Gethsemane preluded victory;
Wilt thou, too, Bloemfontein breed liberty?
'They met at Bloemfontein for rights to fight,'
Historian Africans in years will write.

Ah! Will the struggle then, the pangs, be done?
Will the battle then be lost, still on, or won?
Tell Bloemfontein,
Fountain of Flowers,
Fort of ours.

BAMBATHA O BAMBATHA

Arise and be our leader
Thou Mqhayi and Ntsikana,
Mafukuzela, Mganga
Rubusana, Bokwe,
And Plaatjie and Mantshonga,
Your company now is Bambatha;
He rests asleep with blest your brethren,
Ye prophets gone, both men and women,
Lift high your Voice, let Africa awaken.
Ye poets of the Race, both men and women,
Roar forth in thunder, Africa to shaken!
Now here on earth were reigned confusion
We see the fruits of fusion.
With mighty voice break ye in music,
Let heaven all resound in thunder!
Ah! Sing ye all till mountains echo;
Yea, sing till earth-born children answer;
Ah! Then will cease our useless wrangling,
And shy our enemies will stand confused,
Arise the gates for us all open!
Awake is Africa and coming

TORRENT OF WORDS!

Raging monsoon!
Gods defying;
Gaunt rocks storming;
Giant trees skittling;
Men's hearts lashing to fear;
Dhlomo, we hail you!
Mighty voice of men gone by, and
Mightier men to come!
Eyes to see in mountains puddles molten gold
Soul to shape for man, ebony and brown, a hold
Bedded in mighty rock of innocence
and sweetness—sweet sweetness,
of maiden's laughter, lilting
laughter, dance and song
blind to tawdry ugliness and wrong.
Dhlomo whose curses shake the
empty fane of artificial might!
Dhlomo whose paeans raise the
edifice of power on power
Buttress'd and bound by honesty and
right
And might, olympic, noble, grand . . .
God's hand to raise the puny band
Of men, immortal by th' artificer
plan'd
Write on, great Dhlomo, Sage
Philosopher and Poet!
Look deeper yet;
Back to your rising gods of days
gone by
Up to the heavens, ethereal, lowering,
Thund'rous or starlit sky;
Into the heart of nature's wonder . . .
part concealed

Into the eyes of maidens—love
revealed
Into the heart of God.
Look up and up, until
Amidst the never-ending, ever-
changing splendor of His
Majesty
You catch
The kiss of God for mortal man

MOONLIGHT NIGHT
By Dhlomo

Shall ever I forget that night of murd'rous pain
When soft thy Voice my life and senses helped retain?
O mighty arm of God it cannot be
~~That~~ I am he on whom calamity
And sharp Thy scorpion rods of chastisement
Have fall'n; who goes in tears, despised, head bent!
Healed, shall I rise
And surprise
With a new story
And songs of glory
Those who think
Your image, sod;
Eyes that blink
And see no God
'Mid Moonlight Night,
God-wrought sight?
Great oracle
A miracle!
Be these Visions and dreams
Of thine, or spells,
Moonlight Night
Virgin bright?
Not dreams or spells
Are these, it seems,
For hark!
And mark!
Turns health!
Disgrace
Inverts to grace,
Like Moonlight Night
Where dark weds light!
Ripe in age
And failure,
A new page

In turn, In stature
I know
I grow,
Like a snake,
I molt, I live again!
My thirst I slake
In fountain new (Ah! Pain),
Weak, cracking clay, a trodden sod,
I drink the fertile healing rains of God,
And blossom!
Feel lissome!
Like Moonlight Night,
Angel bright!
O Holy mystery it cannot be
That I am he on whom grim tragedy
And sour thy aching thongs of punishment
Once fell, who were in tears, despised, head bent!

SOUND THE DRUM!

Sound the drum
Boom!
Boom!
Beat! Beat! Beat
Strive!
Strive!
Do or die!

Praise ye, raise them!
Praise the Spirits!
Sing ye, sing them!
Sing our fathers!
The drum the voice of war!
A whole no parts doth mar!
One tone without a jar!
It stirs up all men's hearts!
'Tis king of battle arts
Of sacred oxen hide,
The drum will ever abide.
It speaks of our great Past,
Of first things and of last.
Despite the oppressor's din,
The day the drum will win!
Brave soul, it calls, fight on!
Strive till the work is done—
The task to set us free;
No docile cowards we,
Souls who will win or die;
And will not cringe nor cry.
The cause needs men will dare,
Hold fast and not despair!
Braves who will lead the masses
Through life's stiff, guarded passes,
And serve the Fatherland,

And gain the Chosen Land.
Though troubles envelop,
Warbling of Africa's Hope,
The drum will set us free!
The drum of unity,
The drum of life says, 'Come!'
O men of might—the Drum!
Yea, 'tis the drum!
(Praise ye, praise it)
Yea fight we will!
(Sing ye, sing them)
Strive!
Fight!
Save the people!
Rise!
March!
Who'll be there?

Not for me the Victory celebrations!
Not for me,
Ah! Not for me,
I who helped and slaved in the protection
Of their boasted great civilization;
Now sit I in tears 'mid celebrations
Of a war I won to lose,
Of a piece I may not choose,
Before me lies
Grim years of strife,
Who gave me life
To gain what prize?
In land and sea my brothers buried lie ;
The message came; they answered and they fell,
With blood and toil our rights they thought to buy,
And by their loyal stand Race fires to quell.
Now that the War is ended,
Begins my war!
I rise to fight unaided
The wrongs I abhor!

I see the flags of peace in joy unfurled,
And think of my position in the world
They say will come.
And I stand dumb
With wrath! Not victory in the battle field
Those precious things we crave for life will yield,
I see them gathered to decide on peace,
For War, they know, will lead to Man's surcease.

But Lord, I am not represented;
My presence there is still resented.
Yet where I'm not!
There Christ is not!
For Jesus died and lives for all'
To him no race is great or small.
And if they meet without the Lord to guide,
They cannot build a Peace that will abide.
The causes of war are Greed, Race Pride and Power,
Yet these imposters sway peace talks this hour
How long O Lord before they learn the art
Of peace demands a change in their own hearts!
I'll fight! but pray, 'Forgive them Father,
Despite their boast and pomp they know not what they do.'
I hate them not; believe I rather
My battle will lead them discover Christ anew.
This is the irony,
This is the agony;
As long as those in power repentance need,
I sit upon the spikes of Wrong and bleed!
Ah! Not for me
The celebrations
The peace orations.
Not for me,
Yes, not for me
Are victory
And liberty!
Of the Liberty I died to bring in need;
And this betrayal my wounds and sears my soul. I bleed.

THE HARLOT

I have no love for you,
You to whom my flower I give
I need your aid . . . I don't care who . . .
For, though poor, I too must live

You call me harlot,
Forget my cursed lot,
'Tis you, yes you
Proud Christian, greedy Boss, you apathetic citizen,
Didst me undo,
Though now my company you eschew . . .
For you retain a system that breeds me—despised denizen

Yet I am Queen.
I choose whom I would choose!
'Tis you, not I, who lose.
I form a chaining breeding link between
The black and white;
And in my way I fight
For racial harmony;
For in dire poverty
We are the same,
Play one grim game.
And colour counts for naught
When men in stark realities are caught,
Their eyes are open and they see
They are alike. For poverty,
Like Capital (or truth and works of art),
Reveals the naked human heart

Call me unclean,
Yet am I Queen!
Your daughters, sons, wives, husbands, sweethearts know
I reign with tears and bleeding hearts they crown my brow!
For I am Queen
Although unclean!

You have built this paradise for those
Whom you call 'Master', you have toiled and died
To prove your love and 'pride of nation'.
You have slaved for crumbs you welcome
Flung at you disdainfully—you have thanked them
For the slavery that is your lot.
From the Cape to deep Limpopo
You have toiled for 'Master Whiteman'.

Begging and pleading is borne to your death.
Hating our colour was fanned with your breath.
Time has outrun you, dying old leader,
Take up your Bible and die!
The world shall know us; we're proud we're black!

The old day is dead for the children of sorrow,
The new dawn is born for the children of freedom;
The new era is here for the children of slaves!
These bow to no man, these beg for nothing;
These stand defiant 'gainst a world of jeering;
These do not plead for their hair and their skin.
The new era heralds the new Coloured leader,
Militant, fearless and firm!

Farewell—rest in peace Old Coloured leader,
Your season of pleading and begging is done,
Move aside for the New Man who knows what he must have,
The man who offers no prayers or excuse.
Rest from your labours for time has outrun you—
Whisper your last prayer and go to your God.

FIRED

Believing life is more than economical
And physical; that there exist realm psychical;
That there will come to pass a time
That men in places high will hear and heed the golden words:
'And as ye would', and feel no crime
All human souls soar happily and free;
Unfettered but encouraged to speak free;
And, struggling, fall and rise still facing high,
Not chained by whims of Power or Wealth (for so
The human soul was meant to be),
Down fawning to vain human gods; but know
There is no power save Beauty, Love and Song,
Remembering what such contacts meant to me
Beneath his roof in days gone past
(Though now all's lost,
And mine the cost);
In memory of things eyes cannot see,
But conscience knows—the things that last—
With parting, malice-free, proud greetings,
I offer these imaginative 'nothings'.
The poor misfortune who have felt the rod,
Exalted stand in this: they have felt God!
Grim hope in lowly truthful hearts like mine doth dwell,
Sustaining from severest blows. And so . . . farewell!

ON MUNRO RIDGE

I will ljft up my eyes unto the hils ==
My heart this sight with exaltation fills
Jerusalem can boast no better sight
For here the veld with glorious scenes is dight,
O sweet miniature Edens of the north!
O glorious homes! Is gold but all youp wealth?
But no help cometh from these hills,
It is a heartless beauty;
How can you rest content so near the hells
Of poverty where Moloch fierce still dwells;
Where children die of hunger and neglect
While City Fathers boast suburbs select.

Two thousand years since the incarnation . . .
Must thousands pas ere Man make submission?
A hill; Christ wept! and cried 'Jerusalem! . . .'
Must we pilgrims still weep the tide to stem?
O vision of the hills! Art thou all dross,
Getsemane, Golgoth a and the cross?

This beauty's not for me! My home is not
My home! I am an outcast in my land!
My country's not my own so—will I fight!
My mind is made, I will yet strike for Right!

I sought sweet peace and rest the sea can teach;
Thought there some inspiration I might find.
My venture and my soul soon came to beach!
Where tearing waves of pain my soul did rend!

Out sailed just then the silv'ry cloud-decked moon!
'Clothe patience, son!' it shone, 'Too soon! 'Too soon!'
Thy deep-thought depths these oscillations wild
Do not disturb: beneath them rollest calm!

Tall peaks, streams, force, you boast—yet art thou mild,
Ozone diffusing Element, sweet balm!
Laboratory of life-giving things!
Deep Beauty whom the poet ever sings!

DROUGHT

Hold still!
You gasping craggy heights, you valleys deep!
Sway not your bushy-bearded hills! Dance not
Nor rail at me with happy drunken sounds!
My seeing eyes see not! Heavy my ears,
With song appalled! Thought claw their ways to birth!
Ancestral Spirits great vouchsafe me power
This beauty fierce to seize and rape and make
My own ;;; to express!

For here in truth is heaven-sculptured land!
Sweet hill on hill piles high to form and mould
This swift dimensionless god-wrought ingot,
This spirit teasing speaking miracle,
With patient ancient homes not built but sprung!
Like jeweled flowers! And poised up dizzy heights!
Our human arts poised up in chains of fungus soil
Of crippling laws and forms have now become
Commercial pantomime, a reaping field
For swollen pandits . . . crude and dumb before
This artless Art, this form defying Form!

Land of the singer and the poet (Praise)!
Land of the artist God-enthroned (Praise it)!
Land of ancestral Afric's Spirits (Sing)!
Land of bold warriors, sages black (Sing it)!

They sit with visions and unspoken thoughts
Deep in their eyes and countenances grave;
And they remember and remember, but
All dumb their tongues. The many things they voice
Are ripples on a deep rich sea,
Unfathomed, chartless, and forever still.
Despite charmed peaceful here there is no rest,
Beginning end or death, but constant birth;
A flowering into never-ceasing maze
Of beauty's silent song as gods compress
Their magic notes into a vale, or touch
The strings into a tingling rill, or swoop
A chord into a bulging hill, or fling
A theme into a scattering coloured swarm
Of winging melody! How gods can sing!
Here where we must
Deceive and fawn, shams and crawl like worms a place
To find, and to die to live! Where crafty eyes
Of gain and power, devour devoid of grace!
Not like thy song do men here fall . . . then rise!
But whence you alight, Things by sweet influence
Flow symphonious in liquid confluence!

But who are these who sweat and toil in song?
Who bent and thin like giant forms?
No slaves are these nor blind. They stoop thought-bent!
Rare diggers they! Who toil without a Lord;
Their overseer but the wealth they seek.
They mine for ore surpassing all gold hoards;
They set a tree to feed those unborn;
They toil to find our navel roots from whence,
Like stars and flowers, will sprout the evergreen
Rich groves of our Race Soul. Full well they know
Who mines the past the future makes secure,
But hush! 'Tis done! the wonder of love's toil!
Their magic excavations, like God's breath,
Have touched the scene into a living whole.
Behold! Mist rises up the vales!

What paradise shines blurred out here?
Republic true! The Tribal Village State!
A land of homes and only homes!
No social institutions dark
To right men's wrongs (wrongs just men, wronged,
Find wrongs just done!), for social work
Itself is crime to meet worse crime.
Not land of classes, castes, is this:
But guardians, warriors and the rest.
In harmony sweet-planned abide.
They seek no gains: in community all held.
They thirst for Goodness, Beauty, Truth . . . the Form
Divine, complete! They seek, but . . . they have found!
Corruption is unknown, and systems of
Correction and reform do not disgrace!
Existence is expression not repress.
They serve a state which is their slave, not lord
Their lord, not slaves they serve: he but their Will.

Here children children's life enjoyed,
Not cheated to adults before
Their hour and minds to grow

. . . .

. . . . lordly men like rock hewn strong,
Not bent nor burdened with small things
Of service, but bred and taught
To wrestle with immensities
And lasting things of nation-wide
Philosophies of racial growth;

Free from disease of flesh and soul . . . .
Moonlight night, vision swarm as we go
Calm and bright, safe from harm, slow as snow!
In the vales of the hills!
In the hills of the vales!

For hills find we mountains of strife;
For rills deep streams of blood and sweat;
For trees the swelling song of woe;
For herds the broken people of the land
For heights and depths the depths and heights of woe,
Where joys of life drip hot with pain;
Where but to live is sacrifice!
Erosion sweeps men's soul to ea,
Denuding life of its root joys!
Abyss bespeak Man's cracking Soul!
The crests are babel towers" mad game—
Towers poised mid fact and faith—all false!
The gulfs swell loud with groaning tones
Of souls wrenched down from heights to depths.
A fog of tribulation spreads,
Engulfs and robes the Wrong-torn land
In phantom-like weird orders crud;Iin
In shames and wrongs veiled fair by law!

Abortive is the issue through Man's sin!
There is no power can stand
This ling band!
Agape burst all the holy graves!
Disturbed Ancestral Spirits rise
And call! A hush falls on the scene!
Obedient smiles the sun! The womb
Of life conceives, and life anew *Begins!*.

Swift wild life tells
The unbroken roaming Urge in all black veins.
But best of all behold the winging birds
Take to the skies in song! It is our Soul!
It lives, it mocks, it sings, it soars! 'Tis great!
'As it began so never will it end!
And never will it last as now it is!
The Dawn comes soon! The Dawn—and you!
Whispered the valley of a Thousand Hills.

Create therefore again,
O lord but let now reign
The beauty that this day my eyes have seen
Mine eyes have seen the glory of the coming of the Lord ;
He is trampling out the vintage where the grapes of wrath
Are stored.
John Brown's body lies a mould'ring in the grave,
His soul is marching on!

THE GIRL WHO KILLED
TO SAVE

Then I'll believe that you're dead
When the twittering of the birds in the sky
And the night shining with the stars of heaven;
When the morning haze and the stars
Which light up the darkness like the moonlight
Have all disappeared forever.

Then I'll believe that you are dead
When the mountains and the flowing rivers,
The north winds and the raging south;
When the winter snow and the dew
Which covered the grass today and yesterday
Have all disappeared forever.

The seeds of Shaka, Hintza, Khama and
Moshoeshoe, Go, Cetshwayo, and the band
Of bards of old, cannot forever live
Oppressed. To slv
Avery they will not yield.
Blood boils as they behold both spear and shield,
We'll and take! if others will not give!

Reflected in his face there stood unfurled
The magic and a story of a world
Forever gone and past!
He seemed the last,
Or one at least, of that great tribal land,
Who knew far greater, sweeter, honoured days
Than we who mimic or adapt strange foreign ways!

These were not slaves to greed or pseudo-progress ways
But freedom knew; found time to wonder and gaze!
This face, this sight, this living art is stroke of God;
Not cramped and measured as the arts we plainly plod.
Lord, I am proud that I am black—so black!

UNKULUNKULU—HIS WISDOM

Unkulunkulu in his wisdom saw
The pains, the trials, the journey long of pomp
And crippling revelries man was to tread
Ere Truth and God he attained—Life's journey's end,
To bind man's wounds in pain and hill the scars
Of rejoicings and orgies wild, to make
Of Africans are race apart and rare,
Ubuntu Nkulunkulu shed on them;
Strong legion hopes; fadeless bloom of Love;

The spirit of stout youth forever green;
Swet effluence of song; the gift to know,
Serve and wait as aid to victory;
The Masitela power the deepest wrongs
To bear, forgive; to smile in woe; to sing
In pain; to laugh when laughter is but mask
To hide the keenest pain, injustice dark;
To forgive who hate, betray, or wreck and hurt,
Using such bitteness of soul as stuff
To build mid ruins of the shattered self;
To do the right, see light, when all is dark . . . .
This was *Ubuntu Nkulunkulu* gave
To them—the purest essence of God-life!
Ubuntu fadeless star, green bloom, heaven's song!
Destined to lead black Africa to triumph!

Ndongeni! Praise! Seed of our fatherland!
Son of ancestors bold, you braved the sea
And dangers great to serve and teach this land
Example of the power of unity.
King's deeds and glory are your glory and
Your dees! His fame and praise, your praise and fame!
The full diapason of that theme—Dick's band,
Can never be complete without thy name.

The beauty and the treasures of your home,
Ndongeni—hear and help!—your progeny
No longer call their own! Your children roam
Despised! Outcasts! And never do they flee!
Upon our visions doubts close like a mask!
Was it for this *Ndongeni* rode? We ask.

Oh time! O Place! O Graves! I call!
Bring back the souls, ideas and all
Beliefs and hopes I held in days
Gone past!

But prodigal, I brought but scars,
Of weapons bent, besmeared with blood!
I cried 'Forgive me, Mother dear!
All I have done is, I have stood!
No gifts bring I, I bring myself!
Yet I, even I, am of thyself!
Who stands not in the van but rear!'

New sons and faces young, 'Poor one,'
Jeered forth again, 'What have you done?'
Said trees and fields, 'Let him alone!
We know! Like us he stood lie stone
When fallen, robbed and crucified,
He might have sunk—Fate he defied!'
I wondered who was it replied,
But felt a Presence by my side!

Why do I waste my time thinking of my
Ambitions when my people bleed and die?
. . . . From now till death I give
And dedicate my entire life to these
Mass struggles of the oppressed,
Everywhere I turn I'm haunted
By the wailings of the wounded,
By the groans of the frustration,
By the people daily hounded

By fear and hunger;
By man-made danger
Of lack of house and peace and pasture;
Of their poor children's life and future;
Whose very laughter
Tells of their slaughter
By vested interest of the Powerful Class
Whose greed has landed us to this morass,
And closed the eyes and ears of countless hosts
To beauty and the Truth.

LIFE IN THE MINES:
GOLI, IN THE LAND OF OPHIR
By Moitsadi

City of Goli in the "State" of Gauteng
in the land of Ophir the southern-most
part of the continent of Africa
My ancestral home
Rejoicing take our hearts
Your new-born democracy sets the expectant
World aglow, with Ophir your name to be

It shall be written OPHIR the land of Gold
Let your will be done cleansed from all stains
I speak of Goli at my ancestral home Gauteng

Goli's night lights glaze over dead mine-dumps
restless corpses which my mother's womb delivered
with some heroic aspects of my mother's bravado
obliterated by people from outside Africa
the nucleus that glitters with Gauteng's gold
Sweat of my enslaved siblings obeying
the slave-owners will from dusk till dawn

I no longer wish to reveal my feelings or take heed
When the chains of exploitation deep in the mines
—Deep in my mother's womb rattle still with pain
But tired of never-ending pain and tired
Of never-ending platitudes straight answers do I need

My siblings chocked by dust and overcome by trickery
Spat on, misinformed, kicked, now and again
Petted yet the aim was one to train them for the privileged
My siblings doing their best to obey and please became
Playthings for the enrichment of the privileged

They stumble and fall as they enter the mines
Buried deep in my mother's womb
Their hands dripping with blood a mark
Of hard work and obedience for another's gain
My siblings yearn for their home where they were free

Tired they bellowed notes of bitterness
But there was no sympathy there
Serving, struggling going to sleep on cement beds
Cold, hard like the stone-cold deadest hell
Piled on top of each other like dead sardines
Snatching their breath broken in pain
Driven to death digging precious gold for someone's gain
To be enslaved is death life is doing things for yourself

Eyes all tears spirit crushed and heart-burns burning
from the half cooked strange food served in iron-tins
They must sit and consume on bug-infested blankets
fear is imminent as sounds of others snoring
on hard-concrete cemented beds made in hell to hurt

The long day's anger and pain from dust and rocks;
deep in my mother's womb there was a livered-boy
they begged; What's the name of our country, what is it?
Obliterated by the thought that lead mankind to marvel
they long for their land, their wives, their homesteads,
their children, their cattle, and all that is theirs
they get naught for their comfort all day all night

The sounds begin again these are sirens at dawn
Plus the thunderous *knob-kerrie* knock at the door
the shriek of nerves in pain made worse by
the hardness of cement beds and pain that grief imparts
Ask again—give us the name of our country—what is it?
The name of your country will be known as Ophir; he murmured

The loud wailing lamentation for enslaved men underground
Their faces split by pain and discomfort that calls on the world
The wordless help, endless burden of sacrificial entities
Those not-free know not their country's name—give us a name
Oh our Ancestors! Forever your strength we need they lament.
Any foe that threatens the name OPHIR will perish
Let our country's name be OPHIR the name South Africa is soiled
Our siblings need the radiance of their ancestral benignity
To spread the benign influence of their ancestors. They plead

MY CHILDREN: YOUR REMEMBRANCE OF ME (I'LL BE GONE SOMEDAY)

By Moitsadi

Remember me and fill your minds
With shining thoughts of me, investigate
A process that cannot be denied outright
Remembering me will be a process
From the glory of remembrance and inquiry
consciously or unconsciously of me your mother

To forget me will rob you of that splendid
Part of me, the umbilical cord-connectivity with you
This joy of the long toil that never ceased
And the strenuous fight which only a mother
Can win, a human fight in a race that stirs
The blood in a mother's aorta during child-birth
With a swifter and warmer glow of divine favor

Some of my unfulfilled obligations
must not rob you of your honored merit
and the recognition of my power
the power that speaks of my blood outpoured
to bring you to this world and protect you
from the sway of unknown burdens

A call to remember me will be a cause at stake
the freedom that calls on the world to remember me
Only you my children must make a vow like a prayer
but never require repayment for my dereliction
At least say 'Mother knelt to pray for our safety,'
or 'She offered her prayer by our cradle-side
at night when crying was the only way to complain

No other method did we know' and 'If she could,
she would have done much more to soothe our pains'
'Mama mama wam, mother dear you cared so much'
This you must say and understand, for the affection
of your mother's heart can never be robbed of its joy
'Lala, lala sana lwam mother is by your side'

This I crooned to you my children and wiped off your tears
Your remembrance of me must penetrate the depths
of your minds and enable me to penetrate the years
gone by even after the trumpet calls me to my grave
Remember that I did what I could to mitigate
your displeasures with no misconceptions at all
I expect no words of contempt from you my children
but reading this will soothe your nerves as you reiterate that
'Mother was finer and more brilliant than Gold'

I do not expect you to ask what afterlife will be
Without you my children or to ask what I'll do
in that ghostly grave with the ranks of comrades
But I will whisper your names to the wind and say
In my solitude; my successes and all my efforts;
A mixture of all things I did for you be remembered
So that my wish to live forever can be fulfilled
perhaps I will create a better world full of peace
and justice for all and life without trials and tribulations
when time for reincarnation stands nigh and furled

IN MEMORY OF NICODEMUS
By Moitsadi

Freedom has come at last to South Africa
Our foes, after rampantly killing my kith and kin
Have got you down too at last, Nicodemus now
conferring in the soil with termites where only *Thakadu*
the Aardvark enjoy meals of tiny creatures crawling
silently in a place where there are no lights or fresh air
where unknown termites burrow peacefully
in their abode underground without interference
where leaves that once waved high on trees now molder.

My brother is tasting the soggy gobs of soil,
the once brittle dead leaves of the peach trees,
of roots from which earth crumbles in dry seasons,
the bees buzzing above disturbing the silence.
There you are Nicodemus stilled and lifeless
I can hear your long meaningless name Nicodemus
sideways smile, produced in your mother's womb
the only biblical name that tells of wisdom
the arch-backed, the left-handedness, this my mother's baby
questioning the history of your name remain a mystery
How can a man be born again asked Nicodemus
the wisest man but Apartheid denied your wisdom

During apartheid era—*Bantu* children bred and battered
By westerners whose myths and mind-controlling assertions,
contradictions, hatred for *Bantu* were put into one cauldron
Poisoned-slices unleashed, there is no bread and no butter
Way yonder in homelands desolate areas
Away from skyscrapers, roads, railways built by Bantu
Apartheid did reveal the lessons of divided we fall
The Deep reverence underlying mind-control weapons,
And fundamentals of hatred calculated scientifically failed
One cannot live by lessons from the enemy's mouth
half-killing or half-mesmerizing or half-teaching

Things done in halves are never done right; said Nicodemus
So may we enjoy complete fruits of liberation struggle
From the jaws of the devil but yet no vengeance
Only blazing and beautified unmatched Bantu power,
though Bantu locations bring again to memory
Those killed and dumped like bags of mealie-meal
Into pre-dug ever ready graves marked for Bantu
Whose dead tissues take root and bind the soil,
We love you Nicodemus and all who died fighting

CHILDREN'S FLYING DOVES
By Moitsadi

Bantu Children looked up the sky
In search of flying doves
A single dove denotes sorrow they yell
Two flying doves bring joy and laughter
Four doves give love they laughed
How children wished for love and joy
And how they mellowed enthusiastically

But even in this hour of soft imagery
Gentle smiles console each little friend
The love and joy that overflows
They condescended, confident in their wishes
And from the fading blue skies above
The end of the day brightens with the evening twilight
Night falls and the images of beauty must end

Before the fading sunset came, a spectacle emerged
And in the twilight, voices wailing past
Wild swans calling "Good children go to heaven
When they leave they say goodbye"
Ubani'gama lako—what is your name the angels will ask
And woe to children that linger and are last
A vivid description of all that matters to children

We'll protect one another when the sun sinks
There where stars shine like Angels, they extol
To those who cry in heaven beyond the skies
God comes to judge and pour blessings
Learn what you are children—behave yourselves
Heaven is full of bliss for those who are good
A vivid description of the children's imagery

If blazing noonday sun shines
Groups of children enjoy the shade of the peach tree
But in that Soweto Location, learning an unknown
Oppressor's Afrikaans language was a curse and scorn
That brought death of peace, joy and love
Behind the tranquil of the peach trees
As children remember: one for sorrow;
two for joy and four for love We'll keep it, they said

BEFORE THE
ADVENT OF WESTERNERS
TO SOUTH AFRICA

by Moitsadi

I can imagine how mother Africa was before
The advent of the Westerners
and yet I cannot build on my imagination
Mother Africa had little avarice they said
And a tragedy of deficit greed—true or false

Ruins upon ruins left bruises and tears all around
Mapungubwe born out of the pursuit of luxury
A mark of civilization second to none;
Indeed, I know Mapungubwe that you acquired
Your greatness through the pursuit of pride in gold
—and yet I cannot build on my imagination
The surplus enough to manufacture
Marvelous objects not out of compulsions

Strange as it may seem Mapungubwe propelled
Civilization to a very high level of prestige
To encourage creativity by Bantu South Africans
who breathed conformity and not greed
incentives multiplied in cattle as reward

Mapungubwe's greatness leaned on more productivity
More prestigious creativity, more prestigious incentives,
To encourage equilibrium between conformity and
Creativity, no cleavages ever clashed with
Bantu values—a constraint eliminating greed

Though I built in part on my imagination thus far
It is the same in the production of beads
Beads that have seen the nature of human nature
Rupture with love and envy; greed and deceit and theft
One end of the spectrum are the scientists
Using raman spectra to analyse Mapungubwe's glass beads

It's the Bantu who manufactured these *vhalundzi vhamadzi*
Translucent beads. Thousands and thousands of beads
Buried in your womb, OH! Mapungubwe
Boasting, reveal your beauty
In red, yellow, green, blue,
White, black, pink and plum
Colors of the rainbow represented also
In this array of colors
People of the world can see for themselves
This archaeological record;
Evidence of Mapungubwe's greatness.

The blindness has left their eyes
Different colors, shapes and sizes found.
What more can be said of your color scheme
Of your grand civilization and pride
Mapungubwe your gold and artifacts were born before Jesus Christ
Since time immemorial you stood your ground boasting

Your beads so sleek, lovely manufactured with pride and love
Not asking help from anyone—from across the vast ocean
Simply priding yourself, boasting about your beads and gold-artifacts
on being the most beautiful beads the world has ever seen
More beautiful than the heavenly stars that shine
Testament of the breathtaking gold, glass, and metal skills
The world stands agape—Your scientific skill distinguished

"Excavate, excavate, gold is galore" someone said
People from across the sea, where no gold exists.
Found evidence of Bantu-South Africa's
intellectuals knack, they found and adored
Bantu South African scientific knowledge of yore
Scholars trained by Bantu in
Calculus
Mathematics
Physics
Chemistry
Not forgetting the Art

Some foreigners tried to deny that which the eyes could see
Spreading false information about your greatness
OH! Mapungubwe, see how fallacies were disseminated
See how their tongues trip on ignorance and deceit.
But your everlasting greatness cannot be denied.
Now, shame the world! Sing *Nkosi sikelela* to Mapungubwe
To overcome that which was concealed from your descendants

Job training for the Bantus only! they must be trained!
Some westerner yelled. A piece of rationalization and deceit,
So as to camouflage Mapungubwe's civilization and greatness
Of the time when others of the western world lived in caves.

OH! Mapungubwe see how their tongues keep tripping
on their ignorance, deceit and shameful deeds
With lessons learnt from the Apartheid regime
they had tried to tie the law without *Ubuntu*

Their experiments at Pelindaba and Vulindaba exposed
they thought the job was done when they extolled that
Bantu people must be put to work for their masters
and obey the wills of their owners or be decimated
but alas, no lies brought them to their goal

MAPUNGUBWE
By Moitsadi

Know what Mapungubwe has offered to world civilization
A highly civilized existence, a political system of organization
Life her progeny spent mining, excavating what they owned,
Guarded and left to Mapungubwe's own devices.
With this high honor devolved upon Mapungubwe—existed
A corresponding responsibility of authority and her great power.

Before the advent of Europeans to Mapungubwe's ancestral home
More than two thousand years of peaceful existence ago
And in harmony her golden artifacts buried in graves for her progeny
Came 1932 a period in question the year Europeans found
Her artifacts and caught her off-guard, unarmed, unprotected
free and free-breathing, unperturbed, trees around her swaying
swinging with the wind kissing nature's fresh-air
They threw her out of compass, her trees stopped swinging

All she had buried, beads and golden artifacts so beautiful saw gallons
Of tears from Mapungubwe's Bantu, asking for no compensation
Tears filled the Limpopo river, caught in a flood of sorrow as Europeans
Dug for her precious gold, with their dirty hands searching her
    mother's womb
Without Mapungubwe's permission they excavated and excavated
O my Mother Mapungubwe: Her person, her private parts in pain
exposed caesarian cuts made searing through her umbilical scar to
reach her gold with the sharpest picks and shovels,
knives and forks they dug and dug
Mapungubwe went limp with pain as they popped out her ancestor's
    best—gold
The wind-dried blood on her pores, the wind-blown tears down her
cheeks caused her to cry privately behind her cupped hands

Mapungubwe's heart missed a beat, leading her to pace around
the gold-laden graves strewn before her; marking her ancestral
   boundaries.
She did finally realize the measure of turmoil caused by Europeans
As day by day they came, to magnify the pain in her ancestor's flesh
   and soul
Her progeny's wasted talents, the artifacts, manufactured beads
Made in South Africa for the Bantu by the Bantu
Oh Mapungubwe—see how her treasures were moved surreptitiously!

See her hill littered with broken pottery and ruins of pitiful massacres
Where once one of her siblings King Sekhukhuni fought fiercely
To protect the mines and the kingdom from European-greed
His might and force repelled them, but some Europeans spotted him
And military campaigns against Sekhukhuni ensued and intensified
King Sekhukhuni's army kept the enemy at bay fighting forcefully

To protect the gold that belong to Mapungubwe and her people
with his stronghold remotely situated a distance away from
Mapungubwe Hill. He succeeded to repel the Europeans
his might and attacks were unmatched by any enemy's bullets

In camp Europeans kept their strategies in check
Their aim was to kill Sekhukhuni, his army and his kith and kin
They failed to kill him, failed to capture him, failed to get the gold.
More than fifty years went by without interference from Europeans
Of Mapungubwe's Hill, her graves of gold and golden artifacts

Day by day Bantu heard King Sekhukhuni extol his greatness with pride
For the coming years ahead, without Europeans causing despair
The path to a distant future was viewed with heavy expectant eyes
They said, it will be perilous since the Europeans bear themselves like
"lice that stay in your blanket to bite you at night when you are asleep"
Dinta tse di lomelang dikobong bosigo o robetse.
But in courage they kept their hearts and in strength lifted their hands up
To break a schizoid and crazed foe; they succeeded . . .

Cattle-looting expeditions increased in numbers and type
European's greed increased exponentially, their looting campaigns
exploded as they hunted Bantu and Beasts in their blood-thirsty raids
Discretion is a better part of valor Sekhukhune's advisors said
King Sekhukhuni's military strategy of discretion helped him greatly
His army ambushed and killed several European cattle-looters

Recovered the looted cattle and returned them to Mapungubwe,s abode
The capital city on a hilltop referred to as Mapungubwe Hill
having failed in their deeds and policies the Europeans
now turned to harassing Bantu daily to prevent them
from sowing their crops these policies too could not destroy King
    Sekhukhuni,
his army or his people

Finally, King Sekhukhuni was tricked and captured
Forced to accept a form of peace treaty By putting a cross on paper
Knowing not what the cross meant nor the contents of the paper
It seemed peace with the Europeans was finally concluded
And normalcy restored, but the Bantu rejected the paper-cross mark
and the peace treaty which was concluded illegally without their consent

In 1877, King Sekhukhuni ratified the treaty and stopped the negotiations
In the interum he was bribed into accepting
To pay a head of 2000 cattle in return for peace by Merensky
a total disregard of African traditions and law showed dangers looming.
His people let him choose between wasted blood and penalty in cattle
As a foil to beat off wasted Bantu blood and dirty European tricks

King Sekhukhuni opted for a penalty in cattle, but was faced with bullets
He was summarily executed in public and his wife sjamboked to death.
His company of 30 generals were all shot at short range and killed
The preacher Rev. Alexander Merensky as an interested interloper
Deceived King Sekhukhuni into accepting to pay 2000 head of cattle

Although King Sekhukhuni and his people obliged, showed respect,
conformed to Bantu tradition as they bowed their heads and listened
"Do you and your people want peace?" asked the European commander
"Yes my lord we want peace" replied King Sekhukhuni
He was immediately dazzled by a rainbow of bullets and executed
How did Europeans play their role, to keep peace,
order and office? If they laid their evil-hearts bare,

A dirty treacherous game, a game marred in deceit—from then on
King Sekhukhuni's people refused to accept European promises,
And withheld Merensky's trust and support
"Would not the world cease to exist if people of Merensky's calibre
recoil from what they teach?" Bantus had more questions than answers

Consequently, Merensky was excommunicated from Sekhukhuniland
'cause his advice lacked the truth and Bantu blood flowed instead
In melancholy, songs of grief still reverberate in the air as they sing:=

"No, we will accept not Merensky's teachings of heaven and Christianity
We shall expose the big lies from cheating European tongues
If not we risk our ancestral land, our cattle, our lives and our people
what good is there that could be better than the ties of blood,
of cattle, of land, of families? Without which there is cause to weep"

Their songs in memory of King Sekhukhuni, his army
And those killed by Europeans are taught from generation to generations

"They should not have died barbarously
They killed our King they killed our leaders
with bullets and words that have no compassion
let us kneel on our ancestors' heads in their graves and pray"
they sing in sad melody of verses and tears of sorrow
the songs emphasized and sung at all festivities

Europeans speak a language of words that spoil and spill blood,
Bantu blood wasted-people stirred and we feel the stir of wonder
Did Europeans seek power or were they just hunting Bantu
for their joy? The Bantu asked.
Or was it just a play game like hunting a game of jackals?
a game or fantasy of oozing blood? In King Sekhukhuland

Bantu People remembered how they marched outwards from their fields
singing about their harvest—before the advent of Europeans
but now they say the Europeans cause more deaths
and celebrate death as they did
when they killed King Sekhukhuni and their leaders

Did Europeans expect to conquer death, or defile their
Foul souls and hands full of Bantu blood-stains
Or did they look for humanity and failed to get it
Did they remember: death takes but replaces the lost
with painful deliveries, sweat and toil,
To replace Bantu wasted blood and tears?

In their noisy-songs of gloom there is dearth
can there not be cattle and peace in plenty? they ask
May we not have the natural calling of death
or shared rains, warmth of land and planted crops
pulsating with healthy spirits and healthy bodies

Warm embrace for all of humankind as they celebrate
not death but loving kindness for Mapungubwe's sake
is all they ask on Sekhukhune and their ancestors' heads
for they knit humankind's *Ubuntu* through perils and dismays

THE COLOR OF MY SKIN
By Moitsadi

The heavy pigmentation of my skin
live upon my lips to extol
the tony-brown ebony skin
to hold the joy of my ancestors who
pumiced my skin's heavy pigment
the sacred love-joy of my brown clay
let the clear light from the sun-baked glory
shine to the passers-by all the memories of yore
Pillars of Zimbabwe, African built—left in ruins

Golden *Tshukudu* the great Rhinocerus
Of untold Mapungubwe gold, on display
in South Africa—Pure gold not illusions.
Abyssinian Obelisks stolen, kept in museums
of the Western world behind bullet-proof glass doors

Pyramids of Africa the Pharoahs' pride touching the sky
Timbuktu, African University of yore educating
world scholars and imparting knowledge
to all inside and outside Africa and to many other countries

Where hands with heavy pigmentation centuries and
centuries ago during the days of yore
Wave high trumpeting for the glory of Africa.
See the United States' dollar the basic monetary unit
of the greatest country in the world—USA
Boasting—about Africa's glory in spirit designed
Shows a clean flame of Africa's pyramid

I am down to my marrow beneath my heavy
Pigmentation of skin, down to my pulsating heart
that filters my soul from the hanging pall of evil smoke
That spells raw smell of dead European cichlid fish
Yet I have no doubt in South Africa's deep unspoken power
That Mapungubwe's net is gold-woven, woven to last forever

Spun of golden threads and strings.
To catch not the cichlid fish
But my grieving ancestors of yore.
grieving over the Westerners' greed; Mapungubwe
will keep my ancestors' flesh in vaults of the sublime
away from nightly torments and strains of tensile stress
which they of heavy skin pigmentation have to endure

Sutures of Mapungubwe's skull bear undue burden
her rites of passage from birth through death
Of her scalpel-torn veins, living but of death
Pluck strange lamentations from the lightening
Sift pure gold from Mapungubwe's ashes

Night errands to the westerners' throne of greed hide
There is too much waste of emotions and myths
Tossing to the hungry purses Mapungubwe's gold
Unrelenting greed till the day's departing gleam
For a cup of gold-dust that fills other's purses

Too painful for Mapungubwe to bear
the severance, of Bantu glittering gold
of wings of the cosmic African umbilical cord,
too vast and heavy the fury of detachment
The pains of loss for a hint of trips unknown
And unfair wars declared on Bantu soil
Indigenous inhabitants with heavy skin pigmentation

To profit by Africa's blood
Aliens torture, murder, forge treaties
Bestial lust for cups of Mapungubwe's gold
Tied to sudden plunges of the foreign flesh
Beyond all subsidence of sense and humility
Bantu will be free from skidding turns

Of falling head-on to *kaleidoscopes* they must defy
Defend Africa's ancient glory and monarchs in ruins
not of volcanic eruption but of shadows of European
greed killer-squads. That will die a sudden death
of pawns. When the heavenly thunder shall beat them
And fling them wide into the ocean

To be devoured, consumed, gobbled down by sharks
In the ileum of sharks they must be stored
For rainy shark-days of coming famine
To be re-devoured, re-consumed and re-gobbled
For the glory and blessings of a heavy skin pigmentation
The hills will still crown Mapungubwe's progeny

The light shall fall upon her like a falling star
With the best golden-crown the world has ever seen
Bantu shall live long to keep Mapungubwe's progeny
Priding themselves of their heavy tony-brown pigmentation
Skin sunlit and evolutionarily branded clean and cancer-free

FOR THE LOVE OF MY COUNTRY
By Moitsadi

Bantu and their Ancestors, though the dividing soil
shall not erode between them, they are one
Woven by the immortal umbilical cords of joy
that feels the throb of their mothers' heart
Heavily laden and cumbered with pains of birth
Though since time immemorial their progeny
learned the speech of freedom during juvenile days
they saw and felt the chains of exploitation

Caught in foes' fires that would not burn their hope
When their descendants were hurled with injustices
Now at last after more than four decades of Apartheid;
oppression, dehumanization, exploitation are all outworn
The future shall bring deeper union, from whose life
and harmony shall spring *Ubuntu's* best hope
for Apartheid nights and their dark days came to pass
when in strife, Bantu men, women and children
perished for their quest and dreams of freedom
Their lives given for a better life to come
When the cauterizing fires of Apartheid are extinguished
and blindness has left the regime's eyes and minds

Hard-eyed before the bright sunrise
Bantu hands turned Apartheid-books' last pages
Let sleeping dogs lie they did warn cautiously
with an old African drum-beat and rhythm
of the stringed *Ukelele* instruments' accompaniment
Dancing to the music of truth and reconciliation
Foes' lips moving in prayer, for forgiveness

While fresh unity dawned bringing knowledge of new birth
Knowledge of springtime and the new season of freedom
Of the sowing of millet and sorghum their traditional cereals
Domesticated by Bantu ancestors during the time of yore
For feasts and libation during all rites of passage from birth to death
That are always celebrated till every cloud is aflame

When time and many years of life cloud their memories
and eyes grow dim with many years seen
Their ancestral spirit run more swiftly
than their feet when liberation survived the blood-spent eras
and friends with musing eyes Bantu freedom they perceived
as bright minds, knowledge and wisdom were received
when peaceful transition in tears of joy was conceived
The transforming rapturous scene? they surely believed

Know that the Bantu and their ancestors in reunions will meet
to remember and heal the last reaches of old wounds
and let their Ancestors at the end of the last rite comfort the dreary
And guide them beyond the tears to happy unending life
Where in peace and ancestral waters the weary
Shall find happiness and rebirth when their long struggles cease

So at this hour and age when Apartheid lies dead
Beyond the pain and havoc it caused
Beyond the menaces of death it caused
Over graves and massacres of eager spirits
On ancestral comforting shoulders Bantu will lean
Ancestral blessings truly they must acknowledge
Then shall the new fires within them kindle
When a Rainbow nation they shall enjoy and admonish
Fathers, mothers, children, all of humankind
The fruits of hope and love shall incredibly awake
As they sing their anthem, *Nkosi sikelela 'iAfrica* and lift
their hearts in loftier spirit together as one nation

APOLOGIA (NKOMATI*)

From Wole Soyinka
By Moitsadi

Doyen of walls,
Your puzzled frown has spanned the gulf
Between us.
Your stoic pride rejects, I fear,
This homage paid across four thousand miles,
Unfleshed at source, not manifested
In the act. Justice glowers in your rejection—
I submit:

Utterances flung like lead shot will never
Forge the chain mail of our collective will.
Only the salt of sweat-bathed palms
Pressed in anger will corrode
These prison bars. Our caged eagles
Wait on flight, their sweet-stern cry to stir
Our air again. Our assaulted patience
Waits in concert.

We wear our shame like bells on outcasts.
The snail has feet—I know; our jury
Shuffles to assemblage on the feet of snails.
These retreats in face of need
Betray our being—no wonder
The traitors steep us in contempt!

An old man of sixty-five ekes out his life
In prison slops. The poet
Strings you these lines, Mandela,
To stay from stringing lead.

WAITING

From Arthur Nortje
By Moitsadi

The isolation of exile is a gutted
warehouse at the back of pleasure streets:
the waterfront of limbo stretches panoramically—
night the beautifier lets the lights
dance across the wharf.
I peer through the skull's black windows
wondering what can credibly save me.
The poem trails across the ruined wall
a solitary snail, or phosphorescently
swims into vision like a fish
through a hole in the mind's foundation, acute
as a glittering nerve.

Origins trouble the voyager much, those roots
that have sipped the waters of another continent.
Africa is gigantic, one cannot begin
to know even the strange behaviour furthest
south in my xenophobic department.
Come back, come back mayibuye
cried the breakers of stone and cried the crowds
cried Mr. Kumalo before the withering fire
mayibuye Afrika

Now there is the loneliness of lost
beauties at Cabo de Esperancia, Table Mountain:
all the dead poets who sang of spring's
miraculous recrudescence in the sandscapes of Karoo
sang of thoughts that pierced like arrows, spoke
through the strangled throat of multi-humanity
bruised like a python in the maggot-fattening sun.

You with your face of pain, your touch of gaiety,
with eyes that could distil me any instant
have passed into some diary, some dead journal
now that the computer, the mechanical notion
obliterates sincerities.

The amplitude of sentiment has brought me no nearer
to anything affectionate,
new magnitude of thought has but betrayed
the lustre of your eyes.

You yourself have vacated the violent arena
for a northern life of semi-snow
under the Distant Early Warning System:
I suffer the radiation burns of silence.
It is not cosmic immensity of catastrophe
that terrifies me:
it is solitude that mutilates,
the night bulb that reveals ash on my sleeve.

OGUN ABIHIMAN

. . . . the act of Samora Machel being more profoundly
self-evident as the definitive probe towards an ultimate
goal, a summation of the continent's liberation struggle
against the bastion of inhumanity—apartheid South Africa.
It is best likened to the primary detonation of a people's
collective will, the prelude to its absolute affirmation
and manifestation. No longer do the natives of Abibiman
ask of the void: 'Will it happen in my lifetime?'
It *has* happened. The rest is history.

FROM OGUN ABIBIMAN I
INDUCTION
Steel Usurps the Forests; Silence Dethrones Dialogue By Moitsadi

No longer are the forests green. Storms
Assail the palm, the egret and the snail.
Bared, the dark heart of a hidden nursery
Of embers flares aglow, a landmass writhes
From end to end, bathed and steeped
In stern tonalities.

The boughs are broken, an earthquake
Rides upon the sway of chants, a flood
Unseasonal, a power of invocations.
Meander how it will, the river
Ends in lakes, in seas, in the ocean's
Savage waves. Our Flood's alluvial paths
Will spring the shrunken seeds;
Rains
Shall cleanse the leaves of blood.

A crop of arms dethrones the ancient
Reign of lush, compliant plains,
A truer fastness than the sanctuary of peace
In sermonising woods, and words, and wool
Over the vision of the ram—the knife
Caresses well, the victim bleats
A final testament of its contentment.

Tearless as dried leaves, whose stalks
Are sealed from waste, we shed green hopes
Of nature paths. Their trails are greener,
They, who violate the old preserves
With tracks of steel
And iron tracks, borne
Southward in His wake, to Veld and Cape
For the hour of our in-gathering.

A savage truth, the steel event
Shall even dislodge the sun if dark
Must be our aid. A savage memory raked
From veils of ashes, bores
Light tunnels through the years.
A horde of martyrs burst upon our present—
They march, beside the living.

Earth
Rings in unaccustomed accents
Time
Shudders at the enforced pace
Ogun
In vow of silence till the task is done,
Kindles the forge

*

Rust and silence fill the thatch
Of Ogun's farmstead. In corners of neglect—
Clods of dried earth, sweatrags, kernels,
A seed—yam's futile springing, a pithless coil
Sunlight seeking, guide ropes, stakes—
A planting season lost. Unswept, the woodflakes
Drift, the carver's craft abandoned. Mute,
A gesture frozen in ironwood, a shape arrested,
The adze on arc-point, motionless. Rust
Possesses cutlass and hoe. But listen . . .

Carillons in the distance. A festal
Anvil wreathed in peals, split by a fervid
Tongue of ore in whiteglow.
The Blacksmith's forearm lifts,
And dances . . .
Its swathes are not of peace.

Who dare restrain this novel form, this dread
Conversion of the slumbering ore, sealed
So long in patience, new stressed
To a keen emergence?—Witness—
Midwives of fireraze, heartburn, soulsear,
Of rooting out, of rack and mindscrew—witness—
Who dare intercede between
Hammer and anvil
In this fearsome weaning?

Huge with Time, a wombfruit lanced,
A Cycle resumed, the Craftsman's hand unclenches
To possess the hills and forests,
Pulses and habitations of men. Swayed
To chimes of re-creation, recalled
To an Origin, a oneness, witness
A burgeoning, a convergence of wills—
Nor god nor man can temper!

The singer's tongue is loosened
The drummer's armpits
Flex for a lyrical contention
For subterfuge has spent its course
And self-acclaiming,
Spurs the Cause to the season of enthronement.
Acolyte to Craftmaster of them all,
Medium of tremors from his taut membrane
I celebrate:

A cause that moves at last to resolution.
Prediction folds upon prediction till
The hour-glass is swallowed in its waspish
Waist, the sun engorged within
The black hole of the sky,
Time and space negated, epochs impacted
Flat, and all is in the present.

Gods shall speak to gods.
Stressed from the graveyards of our deities
Ogun goes to let ambrosia from profaning gods,
From skins of curd and sea-blue veins
To stir that claimed divinity of mind and limb
Whose prostrate planet is Abibiman—
A black endowment since the cosmos spewed
Forth is tortured galaxies?

Let gods contend with gods.
All claims shall stand, till tested.
For we shall speak no more of rights
To the unborn bequeathed, nor will
To future hopes
The urgent mandates of our present.

Our vow of silence consecrates the act
For all, breaks the spell of feeble,
Cold resolve in Dialogue's illusion.
The sorcerers' wands are broken, weavers
Of consolation in the crystal glass
Of fractured sights.
Oh distanced statesmen, conciliators
Soon snared in slight cocoons of words!
Will you make a gift of gab to swollen tongues
Broken on the boot, and make their muteness
Proof of cravings for a Dialogue?

Sanctions followed Dialogue, games
Of time-pleading.
And Sharpeville followed Dialogue
And Dialogue
Chased its tail, a dogged dog
Dodging the febrile barks
Of Protest
Always from beyond the fence.
Sharpeville
Bared its teeth, and *that*

Proved no sleeping dog
Though the kind world let it lie.

Ogun is the tale that wags the dog
All dogs, and all have had their day.
For Dialogue
Dried up in the home of Protestations.
Sanctions
Fell to seductive ploys of Interests
Twin to dry-eyed arts of Expediency.
Diplomacy
Ran aground on Southern Reefs . . .

Pleas are ended in the Court of Rights. Hope
Has fled the Cape miscalled—Good Hope.

We speak no more of mind or grace denied
Armed in secret knowledge as of old.
In time of race, no beauty slights the duiker's
In time of strength, the elephant stands alone
In time of hunt, the lion's grace is holy
In time of flight, the egret mocks the envious
In time of strife, none vies with Him
Of seven paths, Ogun, who to right a wrong
Emptied reservoirs of blood in heaven
Yet raged with thirst—I read
His savage beauty on black brows.
In depths of molten bronze aflame
Beyond their eyes' fixated distances—
And tremble!